View From the Mountain Top
The Vision of Global Harmony
by
Seymour Lessans

I0123436

View From the Mountaintop: The Vision of Global Harmony

Seymour Lessans

Published by Safeworld Publishing Company, 2022.

ISBN: 978-1-954284-10-4 (EPUB)
ISBN: 978-1-954284-15-9 (Paperback)
ISBN: 978-1-954284-23-4 (Adobe PDF)
Safeworld Publishing Company

Table of Contents

Chapter 1 | THE WAGER 1

Chapter 2 | THE MAGIC ELIXIR 27

Chapter 3 | MARRIAGE 43

Chapter 4 | CHILDREN 65

Chapter 5 | EDUCATION 79

Chapter 6 | THE DISPLACED 103

Chapter 7 | IMMORTALITY 119

TO ALL MANKIND

A NOTE TO THE READER

In view of the fact that the first chapter must be studied thoroughly before any other reading is done, not only because it is a key that will unlock a door to the greatest treasure in the history of mankind (the long-awaited GOLDEN AGE that has been hoped and prayed for since time immemorial), but also because chapters two to six, though much easier, will not make any sense otherwise, I am urging the reader to refrain from opening the book at random. You will know why this is necessary soon enough. However, should you find this chapter a little difficult, don't be discouraged from continuing simply because what follows will help you understand it much better the second time around.

When you have finally grasped the full significance and magnitude of this apparently brief work (ten years in the making) by reading it at least twice, and further realize there has never been, and will never be, another like it because of what is undeniably achieved, you will treasure it throughout your entire life.

Chapter 1
THE WAGER

"Eureka!!" shouted Larry at the top of his lungs after five years of unremitted thought, "I have found it at last! But who is going to believe me?" "I know," he thought to himself, "I'll call Jim, he's the most skeptical guy in the world. If I can convince him, I won't have a bit of trouble with others. Besides, he's on vacation, which will give me ample time."

That night, he stayed up very late reviewing all the facts to make sure there were no mistakes. Knowing that Jim would call him a crackpot when hearing what he had discovered, he planned to trap his friend's gambling spirit into betting $50,000. So the next day, after phoning, he went over.

"Well, Larry, what is so urgent, and what is the mystery?"

"I have discovered that the long-awaited Messiah (the solution to all our problems) is nothing other than a psychological law of man's nature which has remained hidden, like atomic energy, until now. By discovering this well-concealed law and demonstrating its power, a catalyst, so to speak, is introduced into human relations that compels a fantastic change in the direction our nature has been traveling, putting a permanent end to all war, crime, hate, prejudice, and

1

the domination of man by man. Very few people are going to believe this is possible."

"You don't say. Is this the big mystery? You know you sound like some kind of kook."

"Just a minute. Isn't it true that the government of the United States is trying to find a solution to war, and don't you hear almost every day that various things are being tried to reduce the number of crimes? If what I claim is so ridiculous, as you imply, or impossible, why do we pay out billions of dollars in taxes to the government for that very purpose — to solve our problems? If the President of the United States made an announcement that a discovery had been made, as I did, would you discount it? Of course not, but because it is someone you have known all your life, someone you are close with, someone you might feel doesn't have the capacity to make such a discovery, you discredit the whole idea, right?"

"Not exactly, but I'll tell you what I'm willing to do. You gamble now and then, don't you?"

"When I think it's a good bet."

"Well, you're so positive about what you think you discovered, you should be willing to make a wager."

"Make it easy on yourself."

"I'll bet you ten grand; is it a bet, yes or no?"

"You're so certain I don't have the solution, why such a small amount? Make it $50,000 and you've got a bet."

"That's a lot of money. In fact, I don't have much more. But before I say yes, answer one question. Who is going to judge whether or not you are right in your opinion?"

"I'll let you alone be the judge. If you say I am wrong, you will simply pick up the $100,000 and be the winner; but if you say I am right, then you will be the loser, is that fair enough?"

"You may have more money than I, but this is one time I think you bit off more than you can chew. I'll go to the bank right now, you too, and we'll give the post to... how about Charlie?"

"Fine."

"I'll explain to him what the bet is all about."

They rushed to the bank, drew out the money, called Charlie, who was willing to join them, but when hearing what it was all about, he wanted to bet ten thousand himself, which Larry covered by going back to the bank. Charlie decided to stay.

"I wouldn't miss this for the world, and if Larry can do what he says he can, I'll lose the money all too gladly as a consolation prize."

They agreed to meet early the next morning, and the time had arrived.

"Jim," said Larry, "do you know the difference between an opinion, idea, conception, theory (these are somewhat related to each other) — and an undeniable fact?"

"I think I do. Two plus two equals four is an example of the latter."

"Would you bet $10,000 you are right?"

"I would bet $50,000... Are you trying to tell me that your solution to the world's problems is not an opinion?"

"You are in for quite a surprise, in more ways than one. But you can kiss your money goodbye."

3

"You haven't won it yet. Besides, you have to convince me it is an undeniable fact, and remember, I am betting the other way."

"Your desire to prove me wrong, not that there's any real connection, brings to mind an ironically humorous situation. How happy would a psychiatrist be if one morning his one hundred patients all phoned to tell him the most wonderful news — that they had been healed overnight as if by miracle and wouldn't be needing his services any further?"

"He couldn't be pleased over losing his income, that's for sure."

"But since he is sincerely trying to make his patients well, shouldn't he at least be happy for them?"

"I should think so."

"Well just imagine how excited and thrilled all governments and religions will be to learn that their services will soon no longer be required because the very things for which these forces came into existence will be prevented from arising or continuing. Isn't it obvious that priests would much rather see an end to all sin than to shrive the sinners in the confessional; that politicians, statesmen, the leaders of the world in general would much rather see an end to all war and crime than to retaliate 'an eye for an eye and a tooth for a tooth?'"

"They should be happy for the welfare of mankind, but they couldn't be pleased to have taken away from them the very things that gave meaning to their existence. The psychiatrist is sincerely interested in making his patients well, but he wants to be the one to do it. Religion would like to see us 'delivered from evil,' but in some manner that confirms what has been looked for — Judgment Day. The Russian government would like to see this new world, but in terms of communism or socialism. Everybody would like to see a great change — 'I have a dream,' said Dr. King (this view from the mountain top), but no one desires any intruders or interlopers."

"Thank you, Jim, I was supposed to say that, not you. Anyway, another ironically humorous situation is this: Those who are endeavoring to correct our ills appear to be cutting off the heads of a diseased hydra; the more psychiatrists we graduate, the greater becomes our mental illness; the more policemen and moralists we have, the greater and more prevalent become our crimes; the more diplomats, statesmen, generals, and armies we have for the prevention of international conflict, the greater and more destruct become our wars. And as an expedient to the situation, we find ourselves being taxed to death while our cost of living steadily rises. Wouldn't you like to see an end to all this?"

"I would, but not if it will cost me $50,000."

"You can have my $10,000, Larry; the government will get it sooner or later, anyway."

"Now, in order for me to win this bet, I must proceed in a manner that brooks no opposition; that is, I must demonstrate that two plus two equals four every step of the way. Consequently, I must call to your attention something that happened in the 19th century, as it has a bearing on the kind of problem initiated by our learned professors and leaders. If you recall, Gregor Mendel made a discovery in the field of heredity, which was presented to the leading professors of his time, who had already established a theory that was taught as true. If they had taken the time to scientifically investigate his claims, they would have found that he was right and they were wrong, but this would have made them the laughingstock of the entire student world. Instead, it was much easier and safer to reject Mendel. However, he did manage, many years later, to receive posthumous recognition.

Today, there exists a theory that is held true, consciously or unconsciously, by the majority of mankind, and because it is absolutely false, a door within a door has remained shut that concealed a thorough understanding of man's ultimate nature, a discovery so fantastic you will catch your breath in utter amazement. To help you see how easy it is for a dogmatic theory to prevent scientific investigation, let us return, in imagination, to the time when man knew nothing about the solar system and listen to a conversation."

"Say Joshua, do you believe the earth is flat, or do you go along with my theory that it is round?"

"Even though most of mankind agree that it is flat, what difference does it really make what I think?' said our philosophical friend. The shape of the earth is certainly not going to be affected or changed, no matter what my opinion is, right?"

"That is true enough, but if the earth is really a sphere, isn't it obvious that just as long as we think otherwise, we are prevented from discovering those things that depend on this knowledge for their discovery; consequently, it does make a difference. Who knows, maybe thousands of years hence we may land men on the moon, which may never be possible without first knowing the true shape of the earth."

"I can understand how a dogmatic theory could very easily prevent scientific investigation. Is this what you wanted me to say?"

"Yes. And now I would like to ask you a very serious question. Do you believe that man's will is free, or not free?"

"I have always believed it to be free, but what difference does it make what I think; the will of man is certainly not going to be affected by my opinion, right?"

"That part is true enough (do you recall the comparison?), but if the will of man is definitely not free, isn't it obvious that just as long as we think otherwise, we will be prevented from discovering those things that depend on this knowledge for their discovery; consequently, it does make a difference."

"Is this the dogmatic theory you alluded to?"

"Yes, but most people do not even know it is a theory since it is preached by religion, government, even education as if it is an absolute fact."

"Well, even though I am betting against what you say you will do, I happen to know that it is a theory; otherwise, there would be no believers in determinism. We don't believe the Earth is flat because we know it is round. But are you trying to tell me that the solution to all problems of human relations is in some way associated with the theory of free will, which you claim is false?"

"That's true, and not only is it false but mathematically impossible to prove true, yet the professors today are even more dogmatic than they were with Gregor Mendel."

"I thought you just made this discovery."

"I knew I was on the right track years ago, but one professor, when I told him of my theory (it hadn't been proven yet) remarked, 'Whatever it is you are working on, my friend, it has to be wrong because you start out with the premise that man's will is not free, and it is free.'"

"But why can't it be proven true?"

"Is it possible for you not to do what has already been done?"

"Naturally, it is impossible for me not to do what has already been done, because I have already done it."

"Well, in order for free will to prove itself true, it must do the impossible. It must go back, reverse the order of time, undo what has already been done, and then show that A, with the conditions being exactly the same, could have been chosen instead of B. Since it is utterly impossible to turn back the clock, which is absolutely necessary for mathematical proof, free will was compelled to remain a theory.

"Although I have admitted it is a theory, there are some philosophers who have proven free will true by establishing that determinism is false."

"That's only because they didn't reason properly. If it is mathematically impossible to prove free will true (this was just demonstrated), is it possible to prove the opposite of this, false? Isn't it obvious that if determinism (in this context, the opposite of free will) were proven false, this would automatically prove free will true, and wasn't it just shown that this could not be done?"

"I'm beginning to understand that the mind of man is quite confused. But why is religion so hostile towards any person who speaks against free will, and why should professors take such a belligerent attitude?"

"The latter considers free will versus determinism nothing but a philosophical discussion equivalent to finding out what came first, the chicken or the egg. It is as I said before; to them, what difference does it really make? But to theologians, God is the creator of all goodness, and since man does many things considered evil, they were given no choice but to endow him with freedom of the will so that God could be absolved of all responsibility. The same thing occurs in society. The government holds each person responsible for obeying the laws and then punishes those who do not, while absolving itself of all responsibility, but how is it possible for someone to obey that which, under certain conditions, appears to him worse? It is quite obvious that a person does not have to steal if he doesn't want to, but under certain conditions, he wants to, and it is also obvious that those who enforce the laws do not have to punish if they don't want to, but both sides want to do what they consider better for themselves under the circumstances. The Russians didn't have to start a communist revolution against the tyranny that prevailed; they were not compelled to do this; they wanted to. The Japanese didn't have to attack us at Pearl Harbor; they wanted to. We didn't have to drop an atomic bomb on their people; we wanted to. In other words, it is an undeniable observation that man does not have to commit a crime or hurt another in any way if he doesn't want to. The most severe tortures, even the threat of death, cannot compel or cause him to do what he makes up his mind not to do. Since this observation is mathematically undeniable, the words 'free will,' which have come to signify this aspect that nothing can compel man to do what he doesn't want to do, are absolutely true in this context because they symbolize what the perception of this relation cannot deny... and here lies in part the unconscious source of all the dogmatism and confusion because man is not caused or compelled to do to another what he makes up his mind not to do. But the words 'free will' contain an assumption or fallacy, for they imply that if man is not caused or compelled to do anything against his will, it must be preferred of his own free will. This is one of those logical, not mathematical, conclusions. Consequently, determinism was faced with an almost impossible task because it assumed that heredity and environment caused man to choose evil, but in reality, so thought the other side, he was not caused or compelled, he did it of his own free will; he wanted to do it, he didn't have to."

"This is getting a little confusing, and I'm one guy you don't want to confuse. Are you telling me that though you know man's will is not free, he is not caused or compelled to do what he does?"

"The words cause and compel are the perception of an improper or fallacious relation, because in order for them to be developed and have meaning it was absolutely necessary that the words free will be born as their opposite — as tall gives meaning to short. The expression 'I did it of my own free will' is perfectly correct when it is understood to mean — 'I did it because I wanted to; nothing compelled or caused me to do it since I could have acted otherwise had I desired.' But the truth of the matter is that at any particular moment the motion of man is not free, for all life obeys an invariable law, which I shall prove in an undeniable manner."

"Thank you. At least now I am not confused. But what actually is the definition of free will?"

"The dictionary states that it is 'the power of self-determination regarded as a special faculty of choosing good or evil without compulsion or necessity. Made, done, or given of one's own free choice; voluntary.' But this is only part of the definition since it is implied that man can be held responsible, blamed, and punished for doing what is considered wrong or evil, since it is believed he could have chosen otherwise. Now it is obvious that a great part of our lives offers no choice; consequently, this is not my consideration. For example, free will does not hold any person responsible for what he does in an unconscious state like hypnosis, nor does it believe that man can be blamed for being born, growing, sleeping, eating, defecating, urinating, etc., therefore, it is unnecessary to prove that these actions, which come under the normal compulsion of living, are beyond control. In reality, we are carried along on the wings of time or life during every moment of our existence, and we have no say in this matter. We cannot stop ourselves from being born or getting older, and are compelled to either live out our lives or commit suicide if not satisfied. Is it possible for anyone to disagree with this?"

"Not unless he doesn't understand, and I do. This whole thing is getting very interesting, so proceed."

"However, to prove that what we do of our own free will, of our own desire, because we want to do it, is also beyond control, it is necessary to employ mathematical reasoning. Therefore, since it is absolutely impossible for man to be both dead and alive at the same time, and since it is absolutely impossible for a person to desire committing suicide unless dissatisfied with life, we are given the ability to demonstrate a revealing and undeniable relation.

Every motion of life, from the beating heart to the slightest reflex action, from all inner to outer movements of the body, indicates that life is never satisfied to remain in one position for always, which shall be termed death. I shall now call the present moment of time or life — here, for the purpose of mathematical clarification, and the next moment coming up — there. You are now standing on this present moment of time called here and are given two alternatives: either live or kill yourself, either move to the next spot called there or remain where you are without moving a hair's breadth, which is death or here. Which do you prefer?"

"I prefer..."

"Excuse the interruption, but the very fact you didn't commit suicide at that moment makes it obvious that you are not satisfied to stay in one position, and prefer moving off that spot here to there, which motion is life. Consequently, the motion of life, which is any motion from here to there, is a movement away from that which dissatisfies; otherwise, had you been satisfied to remain here in this one position, you would never have moved to there. Since the motion of life constantly moves away from here to there, which is an expression of dissatisfaction, it must obviously move constantly in the direction of satisfaction. But let us go a step further."

"Is this step further additional clarification, I hope?"

"It is. Suppose you were taken prisoner in wartime for espionage and condemned to death but mercifully given a choice between two exits: A is the painless hemlock of Socrates, while B is death by having your head held under water. Is it humanly possible to prefer exit B if A is offered as an alternative?"

"You know you haven't given me any choice."

"But if your will is free, you should be able to choose B just as well as A. The reason you are confused is because the word choice is very misleading for it assumes that man has two or more possibilities, but in reality this is a delusion because the direction of life, always moving towards satisfaction, compels him to prefer of differences what he considers better for himself, and when two or more alternatives are presented, he is compelled, by his very nature, to prefer not that one which is considered by him worse, but what gives every indication of being better for the particular set of circumstances involved. The purpose of thinking things through very carefully is to avoid, as much as possible, making a mistake, which is hindsight recognition of what should have been done where the unfavorable reactions of others are concerned. The purpose of choosing is to compare meaningful differences to decide which alternative is preferable. A and B, representing small or large differences (which include the blame, criticism, and punishment that could follow in the wake of certain preferences), are compared. The comparison is absolutely necessary to know which is preferable. The difference, which is considered favorable, regardless of the reason, is the compulsion of greater satisfaction desire is forced to take, which makes one of them an impossible choice in this comparison because it gives less satisfaction under the circumstances. Consequently, since B is an impossible choice, man is not free to choose A."

"I agree with all this, but where is the connection?"

"Just hold your pants on. How many times in your life have you remarked, 'You give me no choice' or 'it makes no difference.'"

"I cannot count the number of times. But . . ."

"Just because some differences are so obviously superior in value where you are concerned that no hesitation is required to decide which is preferable, while other differences need a more careful consideration, doesn't change the direction of life, which moves always towards satisfaction. The truth of the matter is that all through life man is compelled to choose what he considers good for himself, but what you may judge good or bad for yourself doesn't make it so for others, especially when it is remembered that a juxtaposition of differences in each case presents alternatives that affect choice. Now, just take careful note of this simple mathematical reasoning that proves conclusively, beyond a shadow of doubt, that will is not free.

Man either doesn't have a choice because none is involved, as with aging, and then it is obvious that he is under the normal compulsion of living — regardless of what his particular motion at any moment might be — or he has a choice and then is given two or more alternatives of which he is compelled, by his very nature, to prefer the one that gives him greater satisfaction whether it is the lesser of two evils, the greater of two goods, or a good over an evil. Therefore, it is absolutely impossible for the will of man to be free because he never has a free choice."

"You have convinced me, Larry, that man's will is not free. What about you, Charlie?"

"Me too, what I understand of all this."

"But for the life of me, I can't see where this has anything to do with what you claim you are going to do."

"You are not supposed to see this yet, but at least we have gotten past the first step. Now, the belief in free will came into existence out of necessity because it was impossible for man to solve his problems without blame and punishment, which required the justification of this belief in order to absolve his conscience. But once it is established beyond a shadow of doubt that will is not free (and here is why my discovery was never found; no one could ever get beyond this point), it becomes absolutely impossible to hold man responsible for anything he does."

"If the solution lies beyond this point, no wonder it was never found. How is it possible not to blame and punish people for committing murder, rape, stealing, the wholesale slaughter of 6 million Jews? Does this mean that we are supposed to condone these evils, and wouldn't man become even less responsible if there were no laws and threats of punishment to control his nature? Doesn't our history show that if man wants something badly enough, he will go to any lengths to satisfy his desire, even commit murder and pounce down on other nations with talons or tons of steel? What is it that prevents the poor from walking into stores and taking what they need, if not the fear of punishment? This strikes at the very heart of all civilization, the teaching of what is right and wrong, for how is it humanly possible not to blame a person for hurting others?"

"I'm well aware of this apparent impasse. Even Will Durant writes, 'Let the determinist honestly envisage the implications of his philosophy,' which demonstrates that all reasoning in favor of free will is the result of inferences derived from the inability of logic to accept the implications. He also brings to our attention that if man were allowed to believe his will is not free, his responsibility would be decreased because this would enable him to blame other factors as the cause. 'If he committed crimes, society was to blame; if he was a fool, it was the fault of the machine, which had slipped a cog in generating him.' I'm also aware that if it had not been for the development of laws and a penal code, for the constant teaching of right and wrong, civilization could never have reached the outposts of this coming Golden Age. Yet despite the fact that we have been brought up to believe that man can be blamed and punished for doing what he was taught is wrong and evil (this is the cornerstone of all law and order up to now, but we are about to shed the last stage of the rocket that has given us our thrust up to this point); the force that has given us our brains, our bodies, the solar and the mankind systems; the force that makes us move in the direction of satisfaction (or this invariable law of God) states explicitly, as we perceive these mathematical relations, that since man's will is not free, Thou Shall Not Blame anything he does."

"You realize how ridiculous that sounds, I'm sure, but there must be some explanation, so I'll just wait."

"To solve this enigmatic corollary, it is extremely important to go through a deconfusion process since it appears that man will always desire something for which blame and punishment are necessary. Consequently, I must repeat what was earlier pointed out, for the purpose of clarification, that it is an absolutely undeniable observation that man does not have to commit a crime or do anything to hurt another, where an alternative is present, unless he wants to. Even the most severe tortures and the threat of death cannot make him do to others what he makes up his mind not to do. He is not caused or compelled against his will to hurt another by his environment and heredity, but prefers this action because at that moment of time he derives greater satisfaction in his motion to <u>there</u> for one reason or another, which is a normal compulsion of his nature over which he has absolutely no control. But though it is a mathematical law that nothing can compel man to do to another what he makes up his mind not to do (this is an extremely crucial point), he is nevertheless under a compulsion, during every moment of his existence, to do everything he does. This reveals that he has mathematical control over the former (you can lead a horse to water, but you can't make him drink) but none over the latter because he must move in the direction of greater satisfaction."

"You have to do better than that."

"In other words, no one is compelling a person to work at a job he doesn't like or remain in a country against his will. He actually wants to do the very things he dislikes simply because the alternative is considered worse in his opinion, and he must choose something to do among the various things in his environment, or else commit suicide. Was it humanly possible to make Gandhi and his followers do what they did not want to do, when unafraid of death, which was judged the lesser of two evils? They were compelled by their desire for freedom to prefer nonviolence, turning the other cheek, as a solution to their problem. Consequently, when any person says he was compelled to do what he did <u>against his will</u> because the alternative was considered worse, that he really didn't want to do it but had to (and innumerable of our words and expressions say this), he is obviously confused and unconsciously dishonest with himself and others because everything man does to another is done only because he wants to do it, which means that his preference gave him satisfaction at that moment of time for one reason or another. But the reason he doesn't come right out and say, 'I hurt that person because I wanted to,' is because the standards of right and wrong prevent him from deriving any satisfaction out of such honesty when this will only evoke blame, criticism, and punishment of some sort for his desires. Therefore, he is compelled to justify those actions considered wrong with excuses, extenuating circumstance and the shifting of guilt to someone or something else as the cause to absorb part, if not all the responsibility, thus allowing him to absolve his conscience in a world of judgment and hurt others in many cases with impunity since he could demonstrate why he was compelled to do what he really didn't want to do. You see it happen all the time, even when a child says, 'Look what you made me do?' when you know you didn't make him do anything. The boy, spilling a glass of milk because he was careless, and not wishing to be blamed, searches quickly for an excuse to shift the responsibility to something other than himself."

"But the boy didn't want to spill the glass of milk; it was just an accident."

"That's true, but why did he want to blame his own carelessness on somebody or something else if not to avoid the criticism of his parents?"

"But isn't it also true that the boy's awareness he would be blamed and punished for carelessness, such as what happened, makes him think very carefully about all that he does to prevent the blame and punishment he doesn't want; otherwise, he could just turn to his parents and say, 'I couldn't help myself because my will is not free.'"

"This is Durant's contention, but your last statement is a superficial perception of inaccurate reasoning because it is mathematically impossible to shift our responsibility, to excuse or justify getting away with something, when we know <u>in advance</u> that we will not be blamed for what we do. Is it possible for you to say, 'I couldn't help myself because man's will is not free,' when you know that no one is going to say you could help yourself? If you try to justify or excuse your action, it is an indication that the person or people to whom you are presenting this justification must consider the action wrong in some way; otherwise, there would be no need for it. If you do what others judge to be right, is it necessary to lie or offer excuses?"

"I agree, it is not necessary."

"It is only possible to attempt a shift of your responsibility for hurting others, or for doing what is judged improper, when you are held responsible by a code of standards that criticizes you in advance for doing something considered wrong by them. They are interested to know why you could do such a thing, which compels you, for satisfaction, to think up a reasonable excuse to extenuate the circumstances and mitigate their unfavorable opinion of your action. But once it is realized, as a matter of positive knowledge, that man will not be held responsible for what he does since his will is not free, it becomes mathematically impossible for him to blame someone or something else as the cause for what he knows he has done, because he also knows that no one is blaming him. Being constantly criticized by the standards that prevailed, he was compelled, as a motion in the direction of satisfaction, to be dishonest with himself and others while refusing to accept his responsibility like a man. But the very moment the dethronement of free will makes it known that no one henceforth will be blamed, he is also prevented from excusing or justifying his own actions since he is not being given an opportunity to do so, which compels him, completely beyond control but of his own desire, not only to be absolutely honest with himself and others, but to assume full responsibility for everything he does. How is it humanly possible for you to desire lying to me or to yourself when you are not being given an opportunity to lie, and how is it possible for you to make any effort to shift your responsibility when no one holds you responsible?"

"But even though this reasoning demonstrates that man cannot desire to shift his responsibility when he knows in advance that no one is holding him responsible, why should this prevent him from taking more easily what he wants when the risk of retaliation is no more a condition to be considered? The boy who spilled the milk cannot desire to shift the blame (I agree to that) when he knows his parents are not going to question what he did, but why should this prevent him from spilling the milk every day if it gives him a certain satisfaction to watch it seep into the rug? Besides, if the father just spent $1000 for carpeting, how is it humanly possible for him to say absolutely nothing when the milk was not carelessly but deliberately spilled?"

"These questions are like asking, 'If it is mathematically impossible for man to do something, what would you do if it is done?' In other words, how is it possible for B to retaliate when it is impossible for B to be hurt? You have assumed that deliberate and careless hurt will continue."

"I still have no reason to think otherwise."

"You will, very shortly. Now take careful note of what follows.

At this present moment of time, you are standing on this spot called <u>here</u> and are constantly in the process of moving to <u>there</u>. You know as a matter of positive knowledge that nothing has the power, that no one can cause or compel you to do anything against your will; and this other, who is standing on this spot called <u>there</u> to where you plan to move from <u>here</u>, also knows positively that you cannot be blamed any more for your motion from <u>here</u> to <u>there</u> because the will of man is not free. This is a very unique two-sided equation which reveals that while you know you are completely responsible for everything you do — since it is mathematically impossible to shift your responsibility to an extraneous cause when no one holds you responsible — everybody else knows that you are not to blame because you are compelled to move in the direction of greater satisfaction during every moment of your existence. Now if you know as a matter of positive knowledge that not only I but everyone on earth will never blame or punish you for hurting me in some way (I am talking of a first, not a retaliatory blow) because you know we are compelled to completely excuse what we know is definitely beyond your control, is it mathematically possible (think very carefully about this because it is the most crucial point so far — the scientific discovery referred to) for you to derive any satisfaction whatever from the contemplation of this hurt when you know, beyond a shadow of doubt, that no

21

one, including myself who is the one to be hurt, will ever hold you responsible, criticize or question your action, ever desire to hurt you in return for doing what must now be considered a compulsion beyond your control since the will of man is not free? (Just hold your question, Jim.) Remember, you haven't hurt me yet, and you know (this is the other side of the equation) as a matter of undeniable knowledge that nothing, no one can compel you to hurt me unless you want to, for over this you have mathematical control; consequently, your motion, your decision as to what is better for yourself is still a choice between two alternatives, to hurt me or not to hurt me. But the moment it fully dawns on you that this hurt to me, should you go ahead with it, will not be blamed in any way because no one wants to hurt you for doing what must now be considered a compulsion beyond your control — although you know it is not beyond your control at this point since nothing can force you to hurt me against your will unless you want to — you are compelled, completely of your own free will, so to speak (which only means that you are not being coerced to do anything *against* your will), to relinquish this desire to hurt me because it can never satisfy you to do so under these conditions."

"Say Charlie, he's never going to win our money this way. Explain it a little differently, will you?"

"In order to hurt another, either deliberately or carelessly, man must be able to derive some satisfaction from this, which means that he was previously hurt and is justified to retaliate, or else he knows that someone somewhere will punish him someday. Blame itself, which is a condition of free will, is a part of the present environment that permits the consideration of hurt because it is the price man is willing to pay for the satisfaction of certain desires; but when it is removed so the knowledge that it no longer exists becomes a new condition of the environment, then the price he must pay to strike the first blow of hurt is completely out of his reach because to do so he must move in the direction of conscious dissatisfaction, which is mathematically impossible. The solution to this impasse is now very obvious because the advance knowledge that man will not be blamed for the first blow of hurt since his will is not free — which enters a condition or catalyst never before a factor in human relations — mathematically prevents those very acts of evil for which blame and punishment were previously necessary as a normal reaction in the direction of greater satisfaction."

"What is the difference between your principle and the one Christ preached... 'Turn the other cheek?'"

"There is a great deal of difference. What you have just heard prevents the first cheek from being struck, which took an untold number of lives as in Gandhi's bid for freedom. Secondly, man must be willing to die in order for turning the other cheek to be effective; consequently, innumerable abuses cannot be prevented, which starts a chain reaction of retaliation. Besides, how is it possible not to strike back when your very being moves in this direction for satisfaction? Gandhi said, 'Kill us or give us our freedom. We will not resist anything you do to us,' compelling, after many were slain, those in power to find more satisfaction in leaving them alone. But the Blacks cannot apply this psychology because the situation does not call for such a sacrifice. How are the Blacks to turn the other cheek when they are underpaid, overtaxed, and judged by the Whites as an inferior race? It was their effort to correct these abuses, not turning the other cheek, that has brought them this far."

"I still can't see how your discovery (I agree that it is valid under certain conditions) can put an end to all war, crime, hate, prejudice, and the domination of man by man when the causes are so deep-rooted and interwoven. In other words, how is it possible to satisfy both Communism and Capitalism, the Blacks and the Whites, the Jews and the Christians, the Catholics and the Protestants, the rich and the poor, the cops and the robbers?"

"You just bet $50,000 that it can't be done, but don't bet your life, or you'll be a dead duck. In fact, I'm really stealing your money, so if you want to get out of this bet..."

"I've heard that before. You're the one who is chickening out. How do you like that, Charlie? He's going to let me get off the hook because his conscience is bothering him, since there is no way I can win. Well, the bet is still on; now what's the next step? Remember, I agree that your discovery is valid, but for the life of me, I can't see how it can correct all the evils in the world."

Chapter 2
THE MAGIC ELIXIR

"Because no problem exists in our relations with each other unless someone gets hurt, and because our children are having their hearts broken and cut out with the knife of unrequited love, which is caused by an unbalanced equation of sexual desire (when the boy or girl loves more, the other desires less), the ultimate problem before marriage obviously revolves around one point — how to compel a boy and girl, of their own free will or desire, to fall mutually in love sufficiently to marry their very first date."

"You must be kidding! You just can't be serious! If you can do this, brother, then I'll know you're from another planet. What do you think, Charlie?"

"He's betting 60 grand, so he's got to be serious."

"Now watch closely. When a boy and girl reach the age of nubility in the new world, with the knowledge of what it means that man's will is not free, they know that it is impossible for any person to desire hurting them when it is known in advance that there will be no blame. Consequently, when a girl finds herself falling for someone, whether it is returned or not (this is the key to the problem which must be worked backwards to understand the solution), she is completely unafraid to offer her body because she knows, just as certain as two plus two equals four, that when it fully dawns on him that she will never hold him responsible for making her pregnant, developing a sexual habit only to leave and never return, for making her fall all the more with no intention of marrying her... I say, when it fully dawns on him that she will never hold him responsible for this terrible hurt when he knows it would be his responsibility, it becomes mathematically impossible for him to desire deflowering her since there is no way he can justify what he knows she must excuse. Could you deflower a girl under these conditions?"

"No, I couldn't, but this still isn't proof of what you said you are going to do."

"I'm well aware of that. Now when a boy discovers, through these mathematical relations, that a girl is perfectly willing to go the extreme once he has won her affection or stimulated her desire sufficiently, he recognizes that there is no advantage, in fact a complete waste of time, to pay her flattering compliments and hand her a line when he knows that he will be compelled, of his own free will, to refuse her body when it is offered... unless he is serious with her. This knowledge completely revolutionizes dating or courtship. Since it is only natural for boys and girls to desire kissing, petting, and fooling around in general, unless restrained by a rigid adherence to the moral code, it doesn't take long before this desire for sexual intercourse is aroused. However, when the boy fully realizes that should he ever get the girl to the point where he would not have any problem getting her to submit, as was just explained, he is forced to take out only the kind of girl that he doesn't want to hurt, the kind who when she offers her body on the altar of love, it will never be rejected. This actually means that when a boy asks a girl for a date, he is saying to her, in so many words, 'Honey, you appeal to me very much, and I am going to do everything in my power to make love to you, but I will never hurt you.' And the girl is compelled, of her own free will, knowing what he wants and knowing that once they start kissing and petting, he will be hurt very much if denied this sexual satisfaction, to accept only the kind of date that will appeal enough so she will not have to reject him when his body is offered. She knows, when accepting this date, that his desire for her will increase only by arousing and satisfying him; and he knows, when asking for this date, that her desire for him will increase when he arouses and satisfies her passion. Consequently, they are given no choice, and when in a fond embrace his hand begins to wander, instead of checking this motion as a girl was compelled to do to feel clean and decent, she only encourages him all the more as he encourages her. Obviously, both of them will become extremely passionate and desire to go the extreme, but she will desire this very much without the slightest fear that he will ever hurt her by leaving; and the very moment they indulge, with or without contraception, they sincerely pledge their love and are married until death do they part."

"Why are they married? There was no license or ceremony pronouncing them husband and wife. And how do you know they will desire to stay together for the rest of their lives?"

"How long would it take a car, traveling at 60 miles an hour, to go 93 million miles?"

"Sixty times 24 hours equals 1440 miles, 1440 miles, which represents one day, will divide into 93 million 64,583 days, and 365 days will divide into that approximately 176 years."

"But how can you know this when the car wouldn't arrive until 176 years later? Suppose the car broke down, had a few flat tires, and maybe needed another driver or two?"

"We are assuming that the car travels at an average speed of 60 miles an hour."

"And you are able to do this just by extending mathematical relations. I am going to do the same thing with this married couple. I am going to set up mathematical conditions that will force them *to prefer* traveling the full length of their lives together without ever desiring to commit adultery or get a divorce, and they will be given no choice because they will want what they see."

"But they are definitely not married yet, remember? The fact that they indulged doesn't make them husband and wife. Besides, you could have young kids fourteen and fifteen having sexual intercourse. Something just doesn't sound right."

"A boy knows that contraception is never one hundred percent sure; consequently, he is afraid that should his young wife become pregnant, this would hurt her parents very much because they would have to assume the financial burden, and it cannot satisfy him to do this when he knows that no one will blame or criticize what he did. This compels him to prefer waiting until he can be absolutely sure that what he does will hurt nobody."

"But a boy and girl don't have to go to the extreme to enjoy sexual contact."

"What difference does it make, just so they will never leave each other. Wouldn't it be an insult to man's intelligence to criticize and blame a marriage celebrating half a century of genuine happiness just because this young boy and girl decided to get married without the ceremony and blessing of a rabbi or priest, without an exchange of rings, without a license granted by others? Criticizing such happiness because this couple didn't conform to the prevailing customs and standards, although absolutely necessary under the existing conditions, is equivalent to criticizing a hand of bridge played perfectly because the cards were not cut by the person on the dealer's right. In our present world, a couple can get married without having sexual intercourse, and can have the latter without the former, but in the new world, it will be impossible to have one without the other because they are one and the same.

Under these conditions, which must come about when the principles are understood, there is no possibility for unrequited love to develop, no chance for any girl to be swept off her feet and lose her virginity out of wedlock, no chance to sin (this should satisfy the clergy very much), no chance for a boy and girl to hurt each other in any way because all the factors truly responsible are prevented from arising. This mating is the holiest of all unions because it is steeped in a feeling of mutual love, a perfectly balanced equation of desire at this moment in their lives.

The belief in free will and the need to blame engendered the suave, smooth-mannered, expertly controlled habits of the conquering male who ensnared, with his captivating style, many an unsuspecting female. It allowed one girl to keep on a string, for an indefinite time, many boys who sought her hand in marriage and who ended up, in many cases, not marrying anyone because she found it difficult to possess what was already hers if she wanted them. It also gave birth to jealousy, which arises from a feeling of ownership that tacitly blames and judges what is right for someone else, while giving unconscious justification to do that of which one has already been accused. This feeling originates in going steady, then grows in intensity from getting engaged to marriage as it now exists. The first two are a down payment on this right to absolutely possess another individual, and the latter is complete ownership. 'I want you' is the meaning of love before this possession takes place; 'I almost have you' is the next phase; 'I have you at last' is the death of love. Why do you think so many jokes are made about this institution if not because it is a sadly humorous situation as it now exists?"

"My hat is off to you, Larry; you really did it! I have to agree that with the application of your basic principle, all the hurt that previously came into existence in premarital relations is prevented from arising, but what about the hurt that already exists? How can you prevent Mary from cheating on her husband with me when she enjoys it so very much? I want to marry her, but he won't give her a divorce. I realize that a couple marrying under your new conditions might never end up like Mary and her husband, but that doesn't help her get a divorce, doesn't stop me from continuing to indulge with her, doesn't stop him from neglecting her, or her from neglecting him, and doesn't change either one of them into what they are not any more, right?"

"Remember, I can't explain everything at one time, so you must bear with me. However, I will take care of this present situation . . ."

"To everybody's satisfaction — Mary's, her husband's, and mine?"

"That's right, just as soon as I show you how automobile accidents must come to an end, and what must happen to our couple when they get married under the changed conditions."

"Your discovery, if it can do all that you say it can, is not a basic principle but a magic elixir, for with it you are changing the baser metals of human nature into the pure gold of genuine happiness for all mankind."

"Get a load of that, will you, Larry? Jim isn't so bad himself."

"That was pretty good. Anyway, the problem of car accidents, or any kind of carelessness for that matter, is very easily solved. To understand how, I will work this problem backwards also.

Imagine an auto accident in which two children were killed, but the parents were unhurt. You were the driver of the other car, you had been drinking (not that this was the cause of the accident), and you were thrown clear. The mother and father are weeping their hearts out, bystanders are sick over the sight, yet no one questions or blames either you or the parents in any way because everyone knows that you and they were compelled to have this accident. But you know you are not compelled to drink and drive, not compelled to pass on a curve or hill, not compelled to recklessly show off and race, not compelled to wander in the direction of an oncoming car... unless you want to, for over this you have mathematical control, and when it fully dawns on you that should you hurt others with your carelessness you will still not be blamed or punished because everyone knows you were compelled, you are given no alternative but to do everything in your power to prevent a situation from arising that gives you absolutely no satisfaction. How do you feel standing around while the parents of these children cry their eyes out with grief, when no one questions or blames you in any way?"

"But Larry," you might reply, "it was really not my fault but the father's; he went through a red light."

"The only way it is possible for the father to blame someone else, or excuse himself, is if someone blames him. Consequently, each person is compelled to be responsible for everything he does because he cannot shift his responsibility when no one blames him. The primary reason we have had such accidents is that individuals were able to extenuate the circumstances, thereby shifting their own responsibility, while being allowed to drive a car when really not skilled enough."

"Does this mean that driving tests will be much more severe?"

"There won't be any driving tests given by others because this allows a person to shift his responsibility to the school that passed him. However, since driving a car under these new conditions becomes an extremely hazardous occupation, each individual must make absolutely certain he knows how to handle a car before he permits himself to drive under the strain of knowing that if he hurts anyone, there is no way it can be excused or justified. This proves that those who carried ample liability insurance were prepared, in many cases, to pay for their negligence. But when it becomes mathematically impossible to blame someone or something else, it also becomes a form of torture to know that you are responsible for hurting or killing another when no one gives you the opportunity to excuse what was done or pay a price to atone."

"Does this mean there will be no more liability insurance?"

"To be held liable means that you are being blamed for the damage that was done, and since you are not to blame, each person will assume responsibility for the damage done to his own car and himself, which means that when you hold yourself responsible for a person's death, you must also hold yourself responsible for all the other expenses he and his insurance company must incur. However, the risk involved for an insurance company under these conditions becomes extremely small, and the premiums will have to come down. Furthermore, to emphasize this once more, driving will become such a hazardous occupation that only the very skilled will undertake it, and every suggestion made to guide the driver in the right direction will be willingly heeded because of this fear that someone, other than yourself (this is the least consideration in the new world), could be seriously hurt. Today we say — 'Obey the laws or else you will be punished. Tomorrow we say — 'Don't obey the laws if you don't want to, but if someone gets hurt as a consequence, it will be mathematically impossible to blame anybody but yourself."

"I liked that, and I agree that under those conditions, almost all accidents would come to an end. But you have a long way to go before you remove all the hurt in human relations. In fact, something puzzles me about premarital relations. In our present world, boys and girls usually find out things about each other they don't like, after going together for a while."

"If either one is worried that this could happen, they will be compelled to do all their checking in advance, and then if they learn something that discourages them, the boy need not ask for, or the girl accept a date. However, you will soon learn that physical attraction, more than anything else, will be the determining factor, and when words like beautiful, handsome, cute, adorable, lovely, etc. become obsolete in our dictionaries, along with their antonyms — ugly, homely, hideous, etc. — the difference between what attracts these fairly young lovers will pass through the eye of a needle."

"But why should these words become obsolete?"

"First, because the use of words like handsome and beautiful is a source of hurt when other people are judged homely and ugly. 'My first daughter is beautiful,' commented a mother, 'but my second is an ugly duckling,' and this poor child had to go through an entire lifetime being judged an inferior production of the human race. Second, because they do not symbolize anything externally real."

"But aren't certain people more beautiful than others, uglier than others, or are you trying to tell me that 'one man's meat is another man's poison,' or that 'beauty is in the eyes of the beholder?'"

"I am trying to tell you neither, although it is true that you might not like what I like. But the latter expression assumes that if someone were to say, 'She is beautiful to me' or 'She is an ugly duckling to me,' that this would be accurately describing a part of the real world. Since it is not, and since the expression 'Sticks and stones will break my bones, but names will never hurt me' is just as false, it is necessary to correct something Aristotle misunderstood many years ago, so that we can put an end, once and for all, to these words that hurt indirectly. It is this that is at the root of a couple's unbalanced desire for each other. She thinks he is handsome, or he thinks she is beautiful, and when the other person is considered of less value, the one looks up while the other looks down."

"Well, what did Aristotle misunderstand, and do you mean that in all these years this was never corrected?"

"That's absolutely true, but I planned to talk about marriage first. What do you prefer?"

"Let marriage wait."

"Well, tell me, do you believe that man has five senses?"

"I know he has; I don't believe it."

"Aristotle thought so, too, but you are both wrong. Let me show you why, but first, tell me, would you call a peach, pear, apple, orange, and potato five fruit?"

"Of course not, because a potato is not grown in the same manner and is therefore called a vegetable."

"Well, the eyes are not a sense organ because they do not function like the other four. The word sense is defined as 'any receptor, or group of receptors, specialized to receive and transmit external stimuli, as of sight, taste, smell, etc.' But this is a wholly fallacious observation where the eyes are concerned because nothing from the external world, other than light, strikes the optic nerve as stimuli do upon the organs of hearing, taste, touch, and smell. It can be easily demonstrated at the birth of a baby that the eyes are not a sense organ when it can be seen that no object, other than light, is capable of getting a reaction from them because absolutely nothing is impinging on the optic nerve, although any number of sounds, tastes, touches or smells can get an immediate reaction because the nerve endings are being struck by something external. The very fact that an infant at birth cannot focus the eyes to see, which has never been adequately explained, is another reason why they cannot be included with the other four, which are in full working order. Furthermore, and quite revealing (this can be scientifically tested), if this infant, immediately after birth, was placed in a soundproof room with the eyelids removed, and kept alive for 50 years or longer on a steady flow of intravenous glucose without allowing any stimuli to strike the other 4 organs of sense, this baby, child, young and middle aged man would never be able to focus the eyes to see any objects existing in that room no matter how much light was available or how colorful they might be, simply because the conditions necessary for focusing the eyes to see have been removed, and there is absolutely nothing that travels from an object to the optic nerve that causes it. Sight takes place for the first time when sense experience (hearing, taste, touch, and smell — these are doorways in) awakens the brain, which then focuses the eyes so that the child can look through them, efferently, at what exists around him. The eyes are the windows of the brain through which experience is gained, not by what comes in as a result of striking the optic nerve, but by what is looked at in relation to sense experience. The brain records various sounds, tastes, touches, and smells in relation to the objects from which these experiences are derived and then looks through the eyes to see these things that have become familiar as a result of the relation. It is a very complex piece of machinery that not only acts as a tape recorder through our ears and the other 3 senses, and a camera through our eyes, but also, and this was never adequately understood, as a movie projector through our eyes. Consequently, all words that are placed in front of this instrument, words containing every conceivable kind of relation, are projected as slides onto the screen of the outside world, and if these words do not accurately symbolize, as with 'five senses' and 'free will,' man will actually think he sees with direct perception what has absolutely no existence. Will Durant wrote, 'If there is an eternal recurrence of philosophies of free will, it is because direct perception can never be beaten down with formulas, or sensation with reasoning.' This is why a mother could refer to her child as an ugly duckling, because she perceives this directly."

"In my wildest dreams, I never thought about this subject. Where do you dig up these things?"

"That's unimportant. Anyway, there is obviously a difference between the shape and features of individuals, as there is a difference between what some people prefer to do, but by having the words beautiful and ugly as slides in a movie projector through which the brain will look at the external world, a fallacious value is placed upon certain specific differences only because of the words, nothing else, which is then confirmed as part of the real world since man will swear that he sees these beautiful things with his eyes, but in reality all he sees are different features, shapes, etc. This so-called beautiful girl is not striking his optic nerve, which then allows him to see her beauty, but instead he projects the word onto these differences and then photographs a fallacious relation.

If a young child, while looking at one type of individual, heard over and over again, 'Look how beautiful!' with an enhancing inflection, and at another type, 'Look how ugly!' with a detracting inflection, it wouldn't take long before this child would be conditioned to desire associating with the first while avoiding the other. But if these girls, presently called ugly, were placed on a planet where no such word existed, there would be absolutely nothing to prevent them from living a normal life because the males there would never judge them in terms of ugliness or beauty, for no such thing exists except as a projection of our realistic imagination. But here on earth, they are handicapped from the day of their birth because they are constantly judged, not in any personal or direct manner, but in a way we cannot so easily correct because we see them through a kaleidoscope of words that transform them realistically into what they are not. Every other word we use stratifies external differences, which cannot be denied, into fallacious standards and values that appear realistic only because they are confirmed with our eyes and our unconscious syllogistic reasoning. The unhappiness resulting from these words is manifold and manifest in the very fact that people develop a complex of inferiority."

"Since I'm not a handsome guy, that word is never directed at me, so I won't care if it becomes obsolete, but how about the others who like to be classified as such?"

"When people begin to realize, first, that these words are not descriptive of reality, and second, that they are a source of indirect hurt for which there will be no criticism, they will lose their desire to use them. You will understand this much better a little later on. Now let me show you what must happen when a boy and girl get married in the New World."

Chapter 3
MARRIAGE

"I still don't quite understand why I can't ask out on a date more than one girl."

"That's just the point, you can if you want to, but under the changed conditions, you won't want to. Remember, you are going to have sexual intercourse very quickly, with or without contraception, and if you left this girl, it would be a terrible hurt to her for which you would not be blamed."

"You know, Larry, for the first time I'm a little worried about my bet because the full force of something just hit me. What you are actually doing is creating a crucible in which man's conscience is brought into full play. He is prevented from desiring to hurt another in any way, shape or form because his conscience won't permit it when all justification has been removed. But I still can't see how you are going to change the economic world to everybody's satisfaction. But I'll wait and see."

"You needn't worry about your bet because there is no way you can win, and I will not accept it. I only made it in the first place just to hold your interest; otherwise, would you have been willing to listen to me solve all the problems of the world?

"You did sound like a crackpot, and perhaps I would not have listened. However, I appreciate your letting me get off the hook. I'm sure Charlie does too."

"I really do, and I was also worried."

"But now nothing under the sun could make me not want to hear all that you have to say, so please continue."

"Now it is extremely important to understand that when a couple, in the new world, consummate their feelings with a complete sexual relation that results in an orgasm, they are going to fall desperately in love and desire each other all the more because this exciting thrill of physical contact is a new experience that has become associated with one particular person to whom they will turn for satisfaction. Soon, each will be absolutely dependent on the other for what the body now craves, and if this were stopped (as happened frequently in the world of free will for various reasons which occasioned the serious consequences of unrequited love) it would be the worst form of torment. Yet there are two individual desires involved, and it is impossible, in the new world, for one person to desire obligating the other not only because this is a form of advance blame (this was not discussed yet), which is a judgment of what is right for someone else, but mainly because it cannot be preferred when it is realized that this would only make matters worse. Therefore, it is important that you understand exactly what advance blame in all its variations is, and how it differs from our basic principle, knowing *in advance* that there will be no blame."

"I believe I already understand. In the latter case, A is prevented from hurting B by knowing in advance there will be no blame, but advance blame is blaming someone before anything is done by judging what he should or should not do."

"Excellent! Well, don't stop now. What are the various forms of advance blame?"

"I can only think of one... telling others what to do, and I can't see any connection between this and preventing a hurt. In fact, I believe it is absolutely necessary at times to tell others what or what not to do so they can't hurt anyone else or themselves, as with children; and isn't it also true that some people have more knowledge about certain things and therefore have a right to make this judgment?"

"There is a big difference between asking for someone's advice and telling him what to do. Besides, when all the things that hurt other people in a concrete, not imaginary, manner are made known (you are going to be surprised as to who is hurting whom), then it will not be necessary to make this judgment because the basic principle prevents moving in this direction."

"What is this 'imaginary hurt' you referred to?"

"The basic principle draws a line of demarcation between hurt that is real and hurt that is not. For example, in our present world if I did not remove my hat in your home you might consider this a sign of disrespect and ask me to take it off, as certain churches do and certain synagogues do not, but in the new world, whether I keep it on or take it off is nobody's business but my own just as long as no one is being hurt in a concrete manner. If I should sit down in front of someone who cannot see because of my hat, I would desire to take it off because the realization that I would not be criticized for preventing this person from seeing clearly, who would never blame me for this, makes me move in that direction for greater satisfaction. But if you ask me to remove my hat when no one is being hurt, except in this imaginary manner, then you are making a judgment of what is right for me, and to satisfy your desire, I must sacrifice my own. This means that all customs and conventions not designed to prevent a hurt to others, must come to an end — unless someone wishes to follow them, which is his business, such as taking off or keeping on a hat — while those that are so designed, as with a traffic system, will continue in existence to help prevent man from getting into a situation where he will be hurting others, for which there will be no justification, no satisfaction. It also means that a person can dress and wear his hair any way he wants because nobody is being hurt except in this imaginary manner, this breaking with custom."

"But it is not imaginary when parents, husbands, and wives hear criticism and ridicule. It is for this reason that a wife will say, 'Honey, wear this tie with that suit, and please cut your hair, you're beginning to look like a hippie.' And what is it that makes White parents dread the thought that their daughter should be seen dating a Black boy?"

"All that you say is true, but when the critics fully realize that they are hurting those who will never blame them for doing what they are compelled to do — when they know they are not so compelled — they will lose their desire to criticize because no satisfaction can be gotten under these conditions."

"In other words, the wife, telling her husband what to wear, is what you mean by advance blame, right?"

"No, because our basic principle prevents her from continuing as before, not the fact that she is judging what is right for someone else. When she sees that there will be no more criticism, it makes no difference what he wears. But advance blame has nothing to do with what our basic principle can prevent, only with what it cannot prevent."

"I'm all confused."

"Telling others what to do when you are not trying to prevent a hurt is one form of advance blame. Asking favors is another. Let me explain.

"If you should say to your wife, 'Honey, bring me some ice water' or 'Will you do me a favor and bring me some ice water?' — both are forms of advance blame because they blame your wife in advance for not doing what you think she should. Mathematical proof that asking favors is a form of advance blame is easily demonstrated when it is realized that no one could possibly do this if he knew, in advance, that his request would be definitely refused. Consequently, he blames the possibility of being disappointed the moment he asks. Suppose your wife says, 'Get the water yourself; what then? Or suppose a father asks his daughter to get him something, and she says, 'I'm much too busy.' Wouldn't he blame her for her desire, which is not to do what he thinks she should? How many parents control their children with threats of punishment, and how many wives and husbands do favors for each other only because they don't want to be turned down when they have a favor to ask?"

"Well, what's wrong with that?"

"Nothing, except I'm going to show you a way of life that is much superior, a way that everybody will prefer, and the only thing necessary to accomplish this is to remove this advance blame. Consequently, the very first thing a husband and wife, in the new world, must be made aware of is that when they are in the mood for love they are permitted to do anything, say anything, wear anything or take off anything, for the purpose of arousing the other's desire, but they are not permitted to touch the other person in any way without being invited to do so."

"And this is supposed to make everybody happy; who are you kidding? When I'm alone with Mary and in the mood, all I have to do is run my hand up her leg, and she gets hotter than a firecracker. What's wrong with that?"

"The same thing is wrong with this as is sleeping together."

"Mary and I already discussed that, and we both want a double bed... if she ever gets her divorce. Something is wrong with your reasoning, Larry, but I haven't put my finger on it yet. This advance blame is certainly different than knowing in advance that you will not be blamed. I agree with the one, and see how hurting a person can be prevented, but I cannot see where advance blame, that is removing it, offers any advantages."

"The reason sleeping together must come to an end is because the moment you buy a double bed, with no other bed available, you are judging that Mary's desire is always to sleep together and blaming the possibility that she may desire not to. Because she may desire steak one evening doesn't mean she wants it always, and if she feels like sleeping alone, you are actually saying to her, 'Sorry, but I want you to sleep with me,' which means that in order to satisfy your desire, she must sacrifice her own. However, when you and Mary have finished making love and desire to sleep together for the rest of the night, this satisfies both your desires, but should she wish to

48

get up and sleep by herself, this is not hurting you and is her business."

"But if I like her to sleep with me, then it is a hurt because it doesn't allow me to satisfy my desire."

"But there are two desires involved, not just yours. To satisfy her desire, she does not ask that you do anything, but to satisfy your desire, you insist that she not only do something for you but do something she prefers not to do. This is pure selfishness, and it is at the root of more divorces and adultery than you can imagine. It is for this reason that all marriages in the New World must have two beds available. Now, the reason you cannot run your hand up Mary's leg is that you can never be sure this is what she wants when you desire it...unless she extends an invitation. Just suppose she is not in the mood when you are; don't we have the same situation as with the double bed? In order to satisfy your desire, which is to run your hand up her leg, she must sacrifice her own, which is for you not to do this at that moment. However, nothing is stopping you from saying the sexiest things to arouse her, or from letting her see just enough to excite her, but the moment she finds herself also in the mood, she will then accept your invitation by making physical contact. Marrying under the conditions described, you will rarely find an invitation by either party that is not accepted. Should it happen, as when a girl has her period, she will simply tell her husband, and then he will wait for her to extend him an invitation."

"What is considered an invitation?"

"You both have indicators that can be read very easily when either of you is in the mood."

"But suppose my wife gets fat and sloppy as Mary's husband did, wouldn't this decrease my desire no matter how much she tried to arouse me; and if I couldn't respond, wouldn't this be a hurt to her for which I could not be criticized; and then wouldn't I be justified in looking elsewhere for satisfaction?"

"A wife and husband will know that should they ever let themselves get into a shape other than what first attracted their mate, they would be hurting the other by denying this passionate, sexual satisfaction. Consequently, when they realize that the other person would never leave regardless of how much this change in physical appearance would hurt, they are compelled to do everything in their power to keep themselves looking like they looked when they first got married."

"That basic principle is just too much. Suppose I desire to kiss my wife all over; is that permitted once an invitation has been accepted?"

"This is your business unless she tells you she doesn't like it."

"Suppose I want her to kiss my body all over?"

"This is not your business, but if she wants to, and you do not mind, there is nothing wrong."

"Some people call this kind of thing perverted."

"I know, and they also call some people beautiful and ugly, but these words will soon become obsolete. Besides, what you do in bed is your business and her business."

"But how can I marry the girl I love when her husband refuses to give her a divorce?"

"You may never marry her, but before I attack the problem of marriage as it now exists, let me show you why all arguments will never arise between husband and wife.

Once they stop telling each other what to do and stop asking favors, a great change takes place. The wife, knowing that her husband will never ask a favor, finds herself asking him if there is something she can do; and he, knowing that it would be taking advantage of her generosity to suggest what he can do for himself, only allows her to do what would not be taking advantage. 'Honey, I'm coming upstairs; would you like the evening paper, some lemonade, or anything?' And he, not wishing to put her to any extra work, thinks very carefully before suggesting what he could have gotten for himself before going up. Since he doesn't want to run downstairs if he is tired, he is compelled to think like never before because he has no one to run errands for him."

"Suppose when they ask that question, the other replies, 'Yes, come upstairs, I want to make love.' Remember, this is something they can't do for themselves, so they wouldn't be taking advantage, right?"

"Completely wrong. She would be willing to satisfy his desire, even though not in the mood herself, but he, knowing this, knowing that no invitation was extended, could not desire to take advantage.

She will desire to prepare the meals that will make him happy because he would never blame her for preparing those he doesn't like, and he will desire to give her every material thing possible within the bracket of his income because she would never complain if he gave her nothing. They would never stand in the way of each other's desire to do things without their partner because this would be a hurt for which there would be no blame, and they would be prevented from taking advantage for the same reason. They would have no reason to argue (this you will understand much better later on), no reason to commit adultery (their passion will always be aroused to the fullest and then satisfied), no reason to leave each other, and every reason to make passionate love all through their lives. Don't think it isn't possible under the conditions described. And when they celebrate their Golden anniversary, perhaps their Diamond, everybody will know at last that God's will was finally done."

"But it is also God's will that I make love to Mary, that she commit adultery, that her husband refuse to give her a divorce; remember, man's will is not free."

"God is building a house of happiness for his children to live in, but it is not yet complete; there are more bricks to be laid. Very soon, however, the roof will be put on, and when it is, no one ever again will be able to do an evil thing, that is, do anything that hurts another. Consequently, when the Golden Age gets officially launched (this might come as quite a surprise), everyone who is married will be automatically divorced, and a couple will remain together as man and wife only if they want to; but only a very few will desire to leave — those who can do so without hurting anybody."

"That's the greatest news! Then Mary and I can get married. When will this wonderful transition take place?"

"Not before all mankind have been taught what it means that man's will is not free, which, if all goes as planned (remember, I am only a son of God, the same as you), should materialize just before the turn of the century."

"But I can't wait that long for her divorce."

"That's your problem. Remember, I don't make the rules; I obey them. Besides, you have no assurance that Mary would still want you even if the transition got started next year."

"I know how much she wants to live with me as my wife. You know… I just got a brainstorm, a terrific idea, so I'm going to ask you to excuse me. Is there much more to tell about marriage?"

"Not really. Certain other facts about the relation between people, which include a husband and wife, will be brought out later."

"I'll give you a call in a few days, Larry, because I definitely am interested in hearing the rest. How about you, Charlie?"

"Let me know when you're going over, and I'll join you."

"By the way, don't you have all that you have been talking about written down somewhere, like a manuscript?"

"Yes, I do."

"Well, how about lending it to me for a few days so I can review the things you told me? I'll take good care of it, I promise."

"You'd better. I intend to get it published just as soon as I write the final chapter."

Jim really had a subtle plan. He met Mary that evening, but instead of going out or making love, he explained what he had learned from Larry about what it means that man's will is not free. "All you have to do, honey, is get your husband to read the manuscript, and I guarantee he won't stand in our way. Here it is."

She stayed up that night till the wee hours studying, and like Jim, she began to see the possibility of getting Harry to give her a divorce, providing she could get him to read the manuscript. But she dreaded going over. However, the next day she was so happy with the thought that she might at last set herself free from the man she refers to as a Abig, fat, sloppy, nagging husband," who every day, when they were living together, would say, "Where are you going, where have you been, why are you late, why didn't you call, why didn't you come home last night? Do this, don't do that, get me this, get me that" — that she began to sing, "Happy days are here again..." She was humming this tune when her husband answered the door.

"What do you want, you rotten whore, and what are you so happy about? You might as well forget that divorce because I'll never let you marry that gigolo, that wife stealer. If you think for one minute that you can ruin my life, make me miserable, you lousy prostitute, and then expect me to help you find happiness, you have another thought coming. When I die, that's when you'll get your freedom, you dirty bitch, so don't bother coming over to see if I have changed my mind. You think I ever loved you? I hate your rotten guts. Now get out of here before I call the police to arrest you for dirtying my steps."

"Wait a minute, Harry; don't close the door yet. I didn't come over to ask that you give me a divorce. I know it is useless. I brought something for you to read that I thought you'd find very interesting because you are a religious person who believes very much in God. That's true, isn't it?"

"You know I am a devout Catholic. Didn't I go to church every Sunday, and didn't I always insist that you join the children and me, but you preferred playing tennis from early morning to sundown. How the neighbors talked."

"What's done is done, Harry, and you don't have to live with me anymore. Anyway, the author of this manuscript has positive proof that God is a reality and that he is going to reveal Himself to all mankind by performing a miracle. He demonstrates how God comes down from heaven in the form of a mathematical revelation and puts an end to all evil in the world. He further proves that no one is to blame for anything because man's will is not free, which makes God responsible for everything."

"Man's will is not free!? God is responsible!!? What the hell are you talking about? Do you mean that God is to blame for your adultery, for my not wanting to give you a divorce because it is against my religion, and because you're a no-good rat that I would like to make miserable? He is to blame, not you, for my hating your rotten guts, is that what you mean?"

"Not exactly, but sort of. It's all here in this manuscript. The theme is sort of a game for two people. I will not blame you for not wanting to give me a divorce and for calling me all those nasty names, and you won't blame me for wanting one. You know, tit for tat."

"Is that what you want me to read? After ruining my life, you don't want me to blame you because God is responsible, and now I should let you off the hook, right? Isn't that what you want? No wonder you like this author, but you're both nuts. You can take that manuscript and stick it up you know where. God is all goodness, and you, a rat born of the devil, want to blame our Lord for your sins, for giving your body to anybody."

"But wait, Harry, don't close the door yet; just one more minute. I'm not blaming God, actually, because I didn't have to do those things that hurt you so much, if I didn't want to, but God made me want to. You see, there was a purpose to all the evil, and therefore, you shouldn't blame me for committing adultery and wanting to marry someone I love very much. I wouldn't blame you because I know that God is truly responsible since he created us without freedom of the will."

"Where the hell did that author pick up all that crap? The Catholic religion teaches that man's will is definitely free. He must be a real goofball, that guy. But he's perfectly right about one thing. I am definitely not to blame because you are to blame. You didn't have to eat my heart out like you did, hurt me to the core, hurt the children by becoming a cheap slut. You did it only because you wanted to, and now I'm going to get even."

"I don't think you quite understand what I'm trying to explain, Harry. I'm truly sorry about all that happened. I could not help falling in love with Jim; it was just one of those things."

"I know the very thing you are talking about, and I'm not blaming you either, but I can't help myself because God is making me make you suffer like you made me suffer. Now get out of here along with that other goofball."

"One second more, Harry. Maybe I'm not explaining it right, but some scientist said it is a fantastic, mathematical revelation direct from the horse's mouth, God himself..."

"Shame on you, Mary! How can you talk like that about our Lord? You will be punished one day for such disrespect."

"Don't take me so literally. Anyway, this revelation is supposed to make everybody happy... once they understand the basic principle. Maybe it is a little over my head, but it still made me happy. However, it can't hurt you to read this manuscript, and since you are unhappy, maybe it will do the trick. Besides, you certainly don't have to agree with the guy if you don't want to, right?"

"Are you concerned for my happiness? Is that why you want me to read it? Well, drown yourself, and I'll be happy. You must have some ulterior motive, and more than likely it is another attempt to convince me that I should give you a divorce. I agree, it probably was well over your head because you never were too intelligent and never got much of an education. In fact, you never even finished high school. My father, God rest his soul, told me you were absolutely nothing except good looking, and that I would be making a big mistake, especially after my little sister checkmated you in 6 moves. He could never understand what I saw in you, and now I really wonder myself. Goodbye Idiot. I'll read the manuscript, though, out of curiosity. Don't bother me again about a divorce."

Despite his last words and all the abuse, Mary had accomplished her purpose, and she felt absolutely certain that it would do the trick. She then phoned Jim to tell him the wonderful news.

Two months later, she got a phone call from her husband.

"Mary, this is Harry. I want you to know that I can't thank you enough for letting me read that manuscript. I've decided to publish it and have already contacted the author. Furthermore, I also decided to give you a divorce... but only on one condition, that is, I want you to come and live with me for the two final weeks. You won't be under any obligation to cook, clean, or do anything. My vacation begins in 8 days, on a Friday.

Be there at 9 in the morning if you want your divorce," and without waiting for an answer, he hung up.

"Jim," Mary shouted happily, "it worked! That was Harry, and he is going to give me a divorce, but on one condition."

"Well, let's hear it."

"I must live with him for two whole weeks. I don't think I can stand him that long, but I have no choice if I want that divorce. When are you leaving on your sales trip to the West Coast?"

"Tomorrow, I thought I told you."

"Can't you postpone it for a few days?"

"Not a chance. And I think he's being very reasonable."

"Maybe so, but I just dread the thought of it."

"I'll be back in two weeks."

"But I'll be with Harry at that time."

"It can't be helped, Honey, but cheer up; we'll soon be married ... legally, like you want it."

The next day Jim left, and 7 days later Mary packed her bags and went back to the same door where, only a little over two months ago, she was called such terrible names by her husband. She really dreaded the next two weeks but made up her mind to stand it. When Harry answered her knock, never in a million years did she expect to see such a complete transformation.

After studying the manuscript very carefully, which he thoroughly understood and realizing that his wife was free to leave under the new conditions, if she really wanted to, Harry decided to get back in shape solely for the purpose of attracting the kind of female that appealed to him. But before exerting himself in this direction, because Mary still appealed to him

58

physically, he thought he would give his marriage one more try, according to the principles just learned. Consequently, he went on a blitz diet and did a number of things to reduce his weight. So, when she saw him standing at the door, it was like seeing a ghost out of the past because the man who stood in front of her strongly resembled the person she fell in love with many years ago.

"Hi Mary," he said very cheerfully. "Let me take your bags."

They had always slept in a double bed, but Harry had arranged a room completely for her. He even sent the kids away to camp. That evening, after the housekeeper left, he asked if there was anything he could do for her, but she simply said, ANo thank you." She decided to put him to a little test because the condition was to stay in the house with him for 2 weeks, so a little later she remarked, "I'm going out for a while, do you mind?"

"I want you to know, Mary, that I loved every bit of that manuscript. It is exactly what you said, 'a mathematical revelation.' Consequently, you don't have to ask my permission for anything, nor do you have to account for your actions."

She walked down to the drugstore, got herself a sundae, and returned. In the meantime, doing what he wanted to do, Harry had put on such a sexy, translucent robe that any normal girl could not help but feel a twinge of excitement. But Mary, knowing that he would never touch her without an invitation, or unless she accepted his, went to her room and didn't come downstairs again until the following morning. This went on for four days. On the fifth, he was really hurting. He was so hungry for a sexual relation that he wondered if he could stay away for the entire remaining time without attacking her, but Mary was beginning to feel the pressure herself since she was used to having sexual intercourse rather frequently. That evening, as usual, he put on his sexy outfit, only this time he lay on the sofa and began to squirm in a manner that made her feel extremely warm, but she felt kind of funny about approaching him. She wanted to make love in the worst way, but she never liked it when her husband hopped on and hopped off. She liked the way Jim made love, kissing her all over while she kissed him, until they were ready to burst with passion. If she had ever kissed her husband's penis, she was sure he would grab her by the hair and call her a whore. Just at that moment, Harry began to say the sexiest things to her.

"You know what I would like to do to you, baby. I would like to open your legs and ___ your juicy little ___ for one solid hour. Then rest for an hour and ____ some more. I would like to make you come about 5 times."

Mary couldn't believe her ears, and she couldn't stand it any longer. She went upstairs to put on one of her flimsy negligees, and for a moment, Harry thought he had lost her again. But in a few minutes, his eyes nearly popped. But Mary still felt kind of funny about making the first contact, so she sat down on a chair opposite her husband and gave him an unobstructed view of her indicator, inviting him to come over.

They made such passionate love that it put their honeymoon to shame, and when Mary got up to go to her room, Harry said absolutely nothing. In the morning, he was in the mood all over again but knew the most he could do was extend an invitation, so he went to her room and, sure enough, when she saw the reading on his indicator, she got in the mood again, only this time she made physical contact first.

When her two weeks were up, Mary was so much in love with her husband all over again that she knew there was no way she could ever go back to Jim. Besides, she missed her children. When he returned from California, he found a note in his apartment explaining everything and then called Larry to tell him the news and that he was on his way over.

"Congratulations! I understand that you're going to have your book published."

"Thanks to you. I'm sorry things didn't work out, but remember, it was inevitable in this particular case."

"I didn't think you were trying to tell me that this must happen in all cases."

"Of course not, but when the transition gets underway, when the knowledge we have been discussing is thoroughly understood by all mankind, every husband and wife will be automatically divorced, that is, free to leave... if they want to under the changed conditions. Consequently, if two people have not been thinking about a divorce, although they may be committing adultery and having arguments, this knowledge will prevent any more concrete hurt in their relations by the realization that they are completely free to do anything desired without fear of blame, which means that when those concerned try to get back in shape and then make efforts to arouse the desire of the other by extending an invitation, it will be accepted. At the same time, they will realize that their partner will be seriously hurt if this sexual desire is not satisfied. Therefore, when all other factors contributing to arguments are removed (wait till you hear what other changes are to come about), and when they see that passion has again been restored, they will not be able to find satisfaction in continuing with adultery simply because all the justification will have been removed. Don't worry about single people like yourself. They will have no problem getting married very quickly in the new world.

As for the husbands and wives who are thinking about, or trying to get a divorce, they will be completely free to do whatever they think is better for themselves, knowing, of course, that no one will blame their decision, no matter how much hurt is involved. Consequently, a husband will find no satisfaction in denying his wife her accustomed standard of living, which means that he will have to earn enough to support two families. However, if he is able to do this and still prefers to leave because he knows he is not hurting his wife or children in any way, then not only is he free to marry again, but so is she. But this kind of situation will be the exception when everybody applies the basic principle and removes advance blame. Furthermore, in a very short time, only the new type of marriage will be in existence.

In our present world, a husband and wife blame each other for any hurt in their marriage because they are unconscious of who or what is really to blame. By revealing what it means that man's will is not free, which releases the corollary or basic principle that no person is to blame, every individual becomes conscious that he alone is responsible for any hurt done to himself by others, just as long as he makes absolutely certain that everybody knows, in advance, that he will not blame anything they do. You are beginning to see the infinite wisdom that governs this universe of human relations through invariable laws when you realize there is not any law that can compel a man to live with and support a woman if he makes up his mind that anything else is better, but of what value is having this law when he, of his own free will, can never desire to leave under the changed conditions. The services of a rabbi and priest during a marriage ceremony don't come to an end because these include the inculcation of a couple's obligations to each other, which is a form of advance blame, but only because the boy and girl, at this stage of man's development, are getting married in a superior manner, which renders this service obsolete. Think further about this immense wisdom (these invariable laws of God). At the very moment that it is revealed what love actually is ... nothing other than a strong desire for sexual satisfaction (as if we didn't know), we are prevented from having more than one sexual partner all through life while being allowed to fall in love with any number of people who could satisfy this passion.

"This whole thing is simply fantastic, incredible! But what about homosexuals?"

"They are free to find a partner without blame. This is their business."

Chapter 4
CHILDREN

"When are you going to show me how war and crime end once and for all?"

"In a little while, but first it is necessary to discuss education and children."

"Is there a way to bring up a child in the new world so the parents will never have a problem?"

"Certainly, but there are no problems unless someone is being hurt in a concrete, not imaginary manner, remember? Consequently, since it is mathematically impossible to blame a child for being born and for the subsequent needs and desires that develop from his nature (because it is now a matter of undeniable knowledge that man's will is not free), we are given no alternative but to prevent what we do not want. But since we are influenced even where the hurt is purely imaginary, our slide rule, or basic principle, sets up a mathematical standard to test all knowledge relating to children who must be guided by their parents until they can be taught what it means that man's will is not free, which would then allow them to assume responsibility for themselves. Therefore, from the very first day of birth, if they are unable to prevent their child from desiring what they feel will be a hurt to himself, or unable to prevent him from not wanting what they think will be for his benefit (both without any form of blame), then it will be obvious that what they like or dislike for him is something not in any way harmful, and exists only as an imaginary fear based upon false knowledge."

"I think I understand that. If, for example, not eating a particular type food is thought to be harmful, then the parents will be compelled to discover a way to prepare it so that he can like it the very first time it is tasted, for persuasion in any form can no more be used as it is a method of blame and an assumption of what is right for this baby. But if they cannot prevent him from disliking this food, no matter how it is prepared, or from liking rock and roll instead of Beethoven (both without any form of blame), then it is mathematically obvious that the harm they perceive has existence only as a figment of their imagination."

"Very good! Anyway, the first problem arises when a mother decides to preserve her breasts and feed her infant with the formula prescribed by the doctor, even though there is no substitute for what the body developed naturally. Though in many cases nothing really serious could happen, as when Durant wrote: 'In the first three months we were guilty of a grave blunder, for we allowed our child to be used as a laboratory for a newfangled form of desiccated milk. It is a crime which many years of parental solicitude cannot quite clear from our memories."

"But that was years ago. Today, the doctors have greater knowledge of the body."

"The hurt I am primarily concerned with is not to the baby, but to the parents. As a result of improper nourishment, the infant starts to cry from, let us say, colic, and before long begins to annoy them by interrupting many moments of pleasurable activities and relaxation. Since they cannot blame him for this, there is only one possibility open: they must try to prevent this desire from arising. However, they cannot prevent the pain or discomfort the baby is already experiencing, so it becomes necessary to quell his cries by either walking or rocking him to sleep. Before long, he is genuinely spoiled, which is a word to describe a habit (not good or bad except that it is annoying), the parents allow to develop and then blame. Consequently, if he is fed with the proper nourishment, the mother's natural formula (but if you think otherwise, this is your business), kept clean, made comfortable so he is not in pain, the only thing that could make him cry is developing the habit of picking him up when he cries. This does not mean that a baby should never be picked up and played with; on the contrary, it could be done often, but only when he is not crying, and providing you don't want to develop this annoying habit."

"I have a nephew who is so spoiled you wouldn't believe it. I remember when he was just an infant, how his mother did those very things you mentioned. But this is really not a serious problem. What's next with our little angels?"

"When they begin to crawl, if they should knock lamps over, scratch furniture or hurt themselves in some manner, we have no one to blame but ourselves. Consequently, we must prevent this without blaming their desire, but when we say 'don't,' 'naw naw,' 'mustn't,' 'stop,' or just pick them up when they're about to do something we don't want, it is obvious that we are blaming them for being in a position where they shouldn't be. We strike the first blow by allowing this, and then strike a second by standing in their way, which makes them resent us. Therefore, to prevent all this, there is only one possible solution without blame, and that is to keep them in a playroom, play yard, or playpen where they cannot desire to do the things which previously required this checking of their motion from here to there.

By the time they walk, they will have learned the difference between play and living quarters without ever being blamed for not knowing. Remember, a spoiled child is one who insists on doing what you don't want but still allow as the lesser of two evils; it is not one who is permitted to satisfy his desires to his heart's content. By preventing his desire from moving in the direction you don't want, he can never become spoiled. By constantly telling him not to do this, don't do that, he will soon desire to do this all the more, which necessitates punishment as a means of control, or spoiling. Which method of the three do you prefer, and have I given you a choice?"

"But there must be some things you cannot control without blame. What about bedtime, manners (teaching children to say, 'thank you' and 'you're welcome' and how to speak and hold their knife and fork in the proper way), smoking, drinking, and all the other things that adults do not want them to do? Durant also says, 'First, use the word don't sparingly,' but goes on to say that 'don'ts are necessary' to a limited degree."

"The reason he feels this way is because he has accepted standards that cannot be controlled unless he denies his own desires from being satisfied. He decrees that his daughter's retiring time should be eight-fifteen at the age of ten, though he admits that 'the law has been broken now and then, as when some genius of the piano was honoring his home.' He prevented her from becoming spoiled by making this 'sacred monastic rule a trifle of surpassing moment' in his philosophy by being 'quietly and inconspicuously resolute' and by not 'condescending even to discuss so absurd a proposal.' He 'turned it aside as a criminal idea.'"

"Well, I can't see anything wrong with that, and you sound like you don't either."

"There isn't anything wrong, except this one thing. He is not considering her desire but his. He believes very much in the expression, 'Early to bed and early to rise,' and if he doesn't assume the responsibility of seeing that she gets enough sleep, she might not be alert enough the next day in school, or, which is worse, might be too tired to go at all. Nothing is stopping him from going to bed at eight-fifteen as an example of how important this is, but he is not ready yet, which means that he is compelled to blame her desire or else let her stay up."

"But in comparison to other parents, I think he did very well. Look how expertly he handled the 'problem that agitates every home.' Most people say, go and do your practice on the piano, which, he says, is a silly phrase, for it suggests, most unmistakably, piano is a bore, practicing is torture; go and suffer; you deserve it. 'We tried another plan with Ethel; we merely offered her the opportunity to learn the piano if she wished; we left it to her choice. But for weeks before putting the question we spoke of the glory of music, and of the high privilege of performing or composing it.' And later, when a plateau came in her progress and she did not want to practice anymore, 'he girded his loins and fought the demons of passion and custom that bade him to command and compel.' You see, he didn't blame her. Instead, he sat down at the piano and practiced her lesson himself. Then he invited her to join him. Rapidly, her pleasure in the piano returned. Now what in the world is wrong with the way he responded?"

"Absolutely nothing when compared with what other parents do; but we are not concerned with what is better, A or B, only with C, which is the best. In reality, he never gave her a choice where the piano was concerned; otherwise, he would have let her hear other instruments and types of music to decide which she preferred. He did not want her to become a drummer, bugler, saxophone player, so he aroused her interest to move in the direction of what would satisfy his desire, and when she didn't practice he blamed her very much, but in an inconspicuous way, for his disappointment, because he set about, in a very methodical manner, to make sure she would not go off again on another tangent. However, he had no choice to do otherwise. His friends and relatives looked up to a pianist and down on other instruments; up to parents who applied certain standards, and down on those who did not; up to classical music and down on rock and roll; up to someone who completed college and down on those who never graduated high school; up to one who became a good swimmer and down on those who did not; up to one who was taught etiquette and down on those who said 'yeah'. But once all criticism is removed — because this is a definite form of hurt for which there will be no blame — then it will make no difference what their children prefer, just so they are happy."

"I agree that parents constantly push their children in a certain direction, and I can see now why this had to be, but if they didn't, isn't it possible that a child could end up doing something less satisfying than if he were psychologically guided as Durant did his daughter? Isn't it possible that she might have become interested in rock and roll at a very early age, only to change later on in life and wish she had studied the piano instead of drums? Didn't she come to feel that 'classical music was a great boon, worth all the trouble that it involved?' Didn't she find great enjoyment in 'understanding why her father was so crazy about Beethoven' when she found herself feeling what he felt 'when playing the Adieu to the Piano?' A father might direct his son to become a professional earning $50,000 a year, or a baseball player making twice as much. Suppose without this guidance, the boy ends up a laborer earning $6000; don't you think if he had a choice, he would prefer his parents guiding him in this other direction?"

"You are assuming that without this guidance, children could end up worse off, but you are completely wrong, as you will soon see. However, let us continue removing all forms of blame."

"Just a minute, Larry. I am not assuming anything. You yourself said earlier that 'children must be guided by their parents until able to assume responsibility for themselves,' right?"

"I did say that, but you didn't understand what I meant. I am guiding children, so they don't hurt others or themselves."

"But if you are guiding them, aren't you blaming them for the possibility of doing other than what you think they should? And didn't you say, 'without any form of blame?' Where is the

71

difference between what Durant did to arouse his daughter's desire to do what he thought was better for her in the long run, and you arousing a child's desire to do what you think is best? Both are forms of blame."

"On the contrary, they are not. Durant guided his daughter to the end he judged was better and blamed her, inconspicuously, for moving in a different direction than the one he picked. He could very easily arouse a child to eat more by putting less on the plate, which blames the possibility that enough might not be eaten. I put nothing on the plate and let the child decide how much."

"But what about candy and cake, liquor and smoking; if you don't put these things on the table, aren't you blaming the possibility that children might desire them?"

"Is it blaming a child if I never let him desire crawling in front of an oncoming car by placing him in surroundings where this could not occur? Because I put an infant in a playpen near a swimming pool, and do not allow him to crawl where he could drown, am I blaming his desire? Would you put poison on your dinner table?"

"Let's not get ridiculous. Drinking, smoking, candy, and cake are not poisonous."

"You might not think so, and I might not, but if some others do, this is their business. Now here is what I mean. If you want your child to eat something, and he doesn't like it, then you blame his desire by trying to persuade him. If you are smoking, and your 4-year-old son asks for a cigarette, you would be blaming his desire if you tell him that this is for adults only. If he wants to stay up beyond 'the year's decreed retiring time,' you blame his desire if you tell him he must go to bed."

"In other words, in order for a person to live in this world without blaming his children, he has 3 possibilities. He must not allow desire to be aroused at all, must give up the things he likes but does not allow his children to imitate (drinking, smoking, staying up late, etc.), or must allow them to choose what they want without giving up anything."

"Very well said. However, when all blame is removed, that is, when children are raised in the new world, parents will be surprised to learn that drinking and smoking are distasteful to any young child whose desire has not been preconditioned with denial; but when it is, he will prefer staying up late even if he is exhausted, will eat candy and cake even when he's not hungry, and will go outside on a cold day without his jacket even though he shivers."

"But isn't it proper to teach a child to say, 'thank you' when receiving a gift, and if he doesn't, don't you blame him by correcting it?"

"Anytime you expect children to act in a certain way, you automatically blame them when they do not. Consequently, they must be taught only by what they see us do. It is humorous to observe that when children receive a gift, the parents, feeling an unconscious twinge of obligation to say 'thank you' because it was expected, shifted the responsibility to their children rather than meet it themselves; but when the obligation is removed because it is a form of blame, the desire to shift the responsibility disappears, the parents will be sincerely grateful without being under obligation, will therefore desire to thank the giver from the bottom of their heart, and the children will very easily imitate. Any person who expects something for what he gives is not generous because he wants to be paid. By removing the blame, he expects nothing in return and gets paid with overwhelming appreciation."

"It appears that removing all forms of blame is God's wisdom made manifest."

"I liked that very much, but don't tell me you're beginning to agree?"

"It's difficult to see this new world in terms of the old without disagreeing, especially when there are so many variations of blame. But there is one form I know you can't remove where these young children are concerned. Suppose a boy, brought up without being blamed, happens to be sitting on a brand-new sofa in the home of your friend when he gets an uncontrollable desire to use it as a trampoline. This is a definite hurt to your friend who does not like this. But if you take the child off, you are blaming him. Well, what's the answer?"

"The answer is very simple. I would take him off and tell him if he does that again, I will have to punish him, assuming he is my son."

"I don't believe it! You actually admitted that in this case it was necessary to blame! Whoopee!!"

"I planned to tell you this anyway, that children might have to live a little longer in the world of free will, but only until they can be taught the basic principle. This is what they must know in the new world to start school. The mathematical standard I set up as a guide had only to do with preventing parents from hurting children. It is obvious that a child could never desire to jump on any sofa once he knows that this is a definite hurt for which there would be no punishment or blame of any kind."

"You're too much, Larry. Just answer me this: Is there any blame where clothes and toys are concerned?"

"Definitely, but that for which it came into existence is prevented from arising. The origin of arguments and fighting between children has its origin in the use of words like beautiful, cute, etc., for these absolutely discriminate against those who do not evoke these expressions, and then when certain type clothes also bring forth a discriminating response, the one who was hurt will become envious, will blame, and will try to compensate in some way. But once these words are removed, once the parents refrain from any outward sign that certain type clothes and physiognomies are of greater value because in reality they are not, the children will never desire to wear or have what their sisters, brothers, and friends have, because these differences are not a source of importance to them... until they see that others value these differences. What difference could it possibly make to a child what kind of dress you put on her, if no one made any comments?"

"Absolutely none, I can see that."

"And what difference would it make to a child what color and physiognomy he has, if no one made any comments?"

"None."

"Then the problem is simply to remove everything from the environment that makes one person feel superior or inferior over differences that are nothing but a projection of our realistic imagination. Where young children are concerned, even the differences between toys arouse envy. One father couldn't understand why his fraternal twins, a boy and a girl, were not satisfied; he with his toy soldier and she with her doll. But soon they were blaming each other for this difference that was now desired."

"You started to remove more blame when I interrupted you."

"Actually, you can do this yourself once the mathematical standard I set up is thoroughly understood."

"But you said something about it revealing false knowledge."

"This also you can very easily do for yourself when you discover that the knowledge you have been taught is true, contravenes the blame being removed. 'Early to bed and early to rise,' as an example, is absolutely false, but it came into existence to justify getting children to do what otherwise could not be accomplished unless parents went to bed early themselves. Getting children to eat certain types of food because these were considered healthier is another example. All these things are part of advance blame, and the only thing that can make parents desire to change, even in this world, is the realization that forcing children to do anything only creates an unhealthy environment. But all the other things that parents try to force on their children, which do not partake of advance blame, will be more easily corrected because this is only done as a result of people criticizing. When this stops — and it will — it will make no difference to parents what their children do."

"But most parents use their children as slaves, so to speak. 'Johnny, do this, do that; bring me this, bring me that.' It is nice to have others work for you, especially when you don't have to pay them. I can see why a husband and wife would desire to remove this advance blame, because it benefits their marriage, which they want to last forever; but I can't see why parents would, when this denies them the satisfaction of doing less physical work."

76

"Let me show you how easy it is to bring this to an end, as well as all prejudice, hate, and disrespect, when we continue to employ this wisdom of God as our guide."

"Before you start, there seems to be a slight contradiction or misunderstanding. Earlier, you said you were primarily concerned with preventing hurt to the parents, and later you reversed it."

"In the former case, I was referring only to spoiling, something the parents allow to develop and then blame the child for."

Chapter 5
EDUCATION

"This wisdom is really nothing other than the knowledge of what it means that man's will is not free, right?"

"Very true, but it was buried deeper than atomic energy and presents problems that are almost insurmountable. Remember, convincing you is one thing; convincing the entire world is something else. Suppose the very people whose understanding it is necessary to reach refuse to examine the facts on the grounds that the discovery could not be valid because it starts out with the premise that man's will is not free."

"But it is not a premise, not an assumption, not a theory."

"I know it and you know it, but when most of the world believes otherwise, they might just close the windows of their mind to any scientific investigation which requires rejecting a theory that has dogmatically controlled man's thinking since time immemorial."

"You may be right. This new world, which looks good, sounds good, and seems theoretically possible in its blueprint form... so far (you haven't shown me yet how to rid the world of war and crime — two most important items) may be just another dream. The early Greeks knew the earth was a sphere, but it took two thousand years to convince men that this fact was true, and even today there are still some who don't believe it."

"Mary's husband was honest enough to admit he isn't interested in saving the world, just in making a lot of money, which he thinks he can do with my book."

"But he still liked what it did for his marriage... I sure wish I had Mary back. I saw her the other day, and she is not the least bit interested in going to bed with me."

"Anyway Jim... to get back on track, I'm going to demonstrate how it is possible to rid the world of all the remaining hurt that exists in human relations, except for that which exists in our economic relations. I shall attack that next to last."

"What is last?"

"Death."

"Your basic principle certainly cannot do anything here, right?"

"That's true, but I have quite a surprise in store for you. Don't ask me any questions now, just wait and see. God revealed something to me. . ."

"In a mathematical manner?"

"That's absolutely correct... it will make you so happy, you have no idea. Now let's continue.

Once a child is taught the basic principle, he is ready for school."

"But some kids might take longer to understand it than others."

"This is true, but it has no real significance. Even if the principle is not completely understood (which it won't be, of course), they will at least know that no one will ever blame or punish them should they hurt others, and the reason for this. Once in school, they will learn more and more and more about what it means that man's will is not free. However, since school is a means to an end, they will select for themselves; the parents are permitted to do or say anything for the purpose of arousing desire to enroll, but the best method is simply to show them what fun others are having."

"I can't see how a school can function without some kind of standards as to what is right and wrong."

"Who said there wouldn't be?"

"You said parents could not set up standards for their children because this blamed them for doing otherwise."

"But this would be only until they are taught the basic principle. There will be traffic regulations in the new world that tell us it is wrong to do certain things because someone might get hurt, and when we realize there would be no blame should this occur, we prefer to obey what might otherwise place us in a situation where no satisfaction can be gotten. Consequently, the school system will also set up rules to prevent anybody from getting hurt, including the teachers, but under the new conditions, everybody will desire to obey these. A child will know that he has to be in school by a certain time; otherwise, this would be an annoyance to the teacher, who does not want any interruptions when the class starts. Therefore, he would make sure his alarm clock is set to give him ample time. He knows he can't depend on his parents waking him, because this blames them should they not, and he also knows they will never insist that he go to school because this blames him should he not. Consequently, he realizes that the responsibility of going or not going is entirely his own business, and if he wants to be rested each day, he will have to regulate his own bedtime according to what he feels he needs. Then, should 'some genius of the piano honor his home,' he might prefer excusing himself, since the guest was more a friend of his parents, rather than stay up late and be tired the next day."

"But suppose he does go to bed late and is tired the next day; what is to stop him from turning off the alarm and going back to sleep? When he awakens hours later, knowing that it would be an annoyance to the teachers to come so late, who would never blame him for this, decides to stay home for the entire day. How is he going to learn anything that way?"

"You are comparing the schools of today with those of tomorrow, and there is no basis for comparison. You are assuming there will be something in school that would make a child prefer staying away, but on the contrary, all children will want to go so badly that they will schedule their time so nothing interferes. To understand why, you must bear in mind that no teacher will ever tell a child what or what not to do, except when someone might get hurt. The parents, also, will never judge what should be studied as an end, for this blames him for not moving in that direction. Since reading, writing and arithmetic are means to an end, all children, without any persuasion, will desire what their parents are doing. But once they have learned to read, they will be shown the various books for their age without having any opinions expressed as to the superiority of one over another, because this is an indirect criticism should they think otherwise."

"Are you trying to tell me that expressing one's opinions must also come to an end?"

"If it can be done without criticizing someone for thinking differently, it will not. Let me go into this more thoroughly by explaining something that was never brought up. Now, when a person asks a question, he is actually saying, 'Will you do me a favor and answer my question?'"

"In other words ... tell me if I'm wrong ... the very moment someone asks a question, he blames the possibility it might not be answered, proof of which is easily demonstrated when not answering makes him angry because he feels foolish. What time is it?... I asked you a question. What time is it?... Are you trying to be funny? I know you hear me, and you are wearing your watch, so why don't you answer? Are you hard of hearing? Is that why you're not answering?"

"Excellent! I couldn't have done better myself."

"Does this mean there will be no more questions asked?"

"Of course not."

"But you said there will be no more favors asked because this is a form of advance blame, and since asking a question is asking a favor, where is the difference?"

"When a boy and girl get married in the new world, they will say to each other, without actually saying it: 'Honey, if there is anything you are unable to do for yourself but need to have done and know that I can do it, it isn't necessary to ask; just tell me, because I'll know you are not taking advantage.' By the same reasoning, you are saying a similar thing to any person to whom you ask a question. Consequently, you were taking advantage of me with your question about the time because you could have answered it yourself by going into the kitchen, where you know a clock is on the wall. However, when you know absolutely and positively that I will never blame you for asking a question, by making you feel foolish when it is not answered — even though it might irritate or annoy me to answer — you are prevented from finding satisfaction in asking all unnecessary questions, which makes you think like never before. The removal of this form of blame completely revolutionizes many things. For example, if I said to you, 'I think so and so will be our next president,' and you made no comment, it would be like talking to myself. If I then said, 'Didn't you hear me?' and you still didn't answer, I would be getting a little angry. But knowing this would make me feel foolish, you answer by saying, 'Yes, I heard you.' 'Well,' is my reply, 'do you agree or disagree?' If you agree, then there is nothing further to talk about, but if you disagree, then I am given an opportunity to criticize your point of view while establishing the soundness of my own. Since criticizing a person for the way he thinks is a form of hurt for which there will be no criticism in return, each individual will be compelled to desire keeping his opinions to himself. But let me show you something very humorous.

Because in this world, many people are made to feel terribly inferior, they have developed the habit of trying to elevate themselves by pushing others down. They use the N word, dirty Jew, uneducated, but they also ask questions the answers to which are already known to them. 'When did Columbus discover America?' 'I don't know.' 'You should know that; it was back in 1492.' The people who do this are disappointed when you know the answer because it prevents them from teaching you something, from showing off their knowledge, and from placing you in an inferior capacity. Consequently, asking these questions must come to an end because it is also a form of criticism; it is a deliberate effort to make a person feel inferior."

"But this would not apply to a teacher in school whose job is to make sure that children are learning properly, right?"

"Wrong. Teachers will design every conceivable kind of written test so a child can find out for himself how he is progressing."

"Isn't it also important for the parents and teachers to know? Isn't that why we have report cards?"

"When this kind of standard is set up, children are criticized for falling short and praised for doing well, which makes some feel inferior to others."

"But you can't completely prevent this feeling. When someone loses in a game of chess, isn't it natural for him to feel that he is an inferior player? Aren't some children just naturally more talented than others, whether in athletics, music, or what have you? There is no question about this difference in abilities."

"No one can deny that. However, if someone should lose in chess, he is at liberty to give the game up completely, if he wants to, or never even start, but when certain standards are set up for him by others, then they push him in a direction he might not want to go."

"But we are discussing the elementary subjects, which are means to any end he might select for himself, and isn't it important for the teachers to make sure he learns these subjects properly so he can move on to other studies?"

"Certainly, but after every lesson they will say, 'Children, up on my desk is a written test on one sheet and the answers on another. Those of you who would like to see how you are progressing can take these sheets home with you.' Now, if any child desires to take this test, this is his business, but should he discover that he has fallen short, there will be no one to criticize. However, should he wish to learn more about any subject he has fallen short in, he will then approach the teacher after hours, who will either help him directly or indirectly, by recommending books on the subject. But under no circumstances do teachers ever approach a child with a question, unless it is to prevent a hurt of some kind. This prevents him from being criticized by the questions teachers and parents ask."

"Parents too?"

"No questions will be asked that are a form of criticism because this is a hurt for which there will be no blame. It prevents him from being made to feel inferior, as report cards do, and it allows him to approach his parents and teachers without any fear whatsoever."

"Will there be homework?"

"Certainly, but not as we know it today. 'Children, those of you who feel you are not learning all that you should may take home this book and review Chapter 4.' Under no circumstances will any child be placed under an obligation to do anything, although he will be prevented from hurting others by the basic principle."

"Will he graduate from elementary school to Junior High, you know, the regular steps he goes through now?"

"There will be no graduation of any kind all through his entire years in school. When he feels ready to transfer to another school (and he will know because nobody will be judging for him, although he will have the tests he gives himself as a guide), he will simply turn in a card with his name and address and will be notified where and when to report."

"Something just doesn't seem right about not graduating. There are certain professions that require a great deal of study, such as the medical field, and if a student wasn't thoroughly tested by his professors before being turned loose, without meeting the stringent requirements, the universities might be releasing a lot of quacks. I assume, therefore, that to prevent this, he would have to receive a diploma of graduation."

"Absolutely wrong. Every student knows that when he leaves school to earn a living, no one will ever blame him, no matter how much he hurts others with his mistakes. Consequently, employers will not have to screen any applicant for a job because they will know he is completely qualified; otherwise, he could not risk taking a position from which no satisfaction can be gotten unless a perfect job is done. But let me show you what harm a diploma can do.

In our present world, a doctor is allowed to treat the sick, operate on them, administer drugs, etc., on the reasonable assumption that when he received his degree, he automatically became qualified. But if he is not, that is, if the knowledge taught was inadequate despite all that he learned, then he is actually permitted by law to risk hurting his patients with impunity, because he is not a quack, not an impostor, not someone who didn't study hard and pass all the necessary examinations, but a genuine healer, and to prove it we are constantly reminded not to consult those who are not doctors. How many times have you heard the expressions: 'He is not a doctor.' 'You are not a doctor.' 'Recommended by doctors.'"

"I can't count the number of times. Almost every day, you hear some reference being made over television. So what?"

"So this... then all tests by others to determine his qualifications are withdrawn (in the new world, that is); when he is not granted this right by the university and state to practice on the bodies of live people... he must determine for himself his qualifications, which brings about a fantastic change. He knows that should anything happen to hurt his patients as a result of what he prescribed, there is no way he can shift his responsibility because no one is holding him responsible; everybody is admitting that he had no choice but to hurt them this way, which compels him of his own free will to be absolutely certain (no opinions, no guessing, no assumption that the drug administered can't do any harm and may do some good if only to satisfy their fears). He must be absolutely certain about everything he does. The great fear that they might get worse unless he prescribes something, makes him, in this world, deceive his patients about his great healing powers, which allows him to be dishonest with himself; but when it becomes impossible to lie to them, since they are not blaming or questioning his ability, he must be absolutely honest with himself and others, which compels him, for the first time, to realize that they could get worse because of, and better in spite of, his treatments."

"Just a minute, Larry. Are you trying to tell me that the medical profession hasn't accomplished anything?"

"Certainly not, but it has gotten completely out of hand only because of the fears people have. Because doctors today are under a compulsion to earn a living like everybody else, it is suggested that we have six month checkups, and that the foreskin be removed along with the appendix and tonsils; and the only proof that these things are of no value for the body is the fact that their removal is sanctioned by the medical profession which lays its arguments not so much on why it is better or healthier, but on who says it is."

"But there are times when it is absolutely necessary to remove the appendix to save somebody's life."

"I don't deny this, just as there are times when a leg must be amputated. But how many times have tonsils and the appendix been removed not because there was any danger to the patient's life, but only because these are considered vestigial organs to confirm Darwin's theory? And what terrible thing will happen to a child if his foreskin is not removed?"

"The doctors say it is healthier. Besides, you are Jewish too, and with us it is an ancient religious custom. It is our birthright."

"I am an earthling, nothing else. As to ancient religious customs, there was a time when the entire body was sacrificed. As to circumcision being healthier, if it were not for many Jews questioning the justification for this operation, the medical profession would never have absolved their conscience with the knowledge that it is healthier, but when this meant millions of more dollars in the pockets of doctors who now could justify getting even those who were not Jewish to spend their money, they were given no choice. However, this is not a criticism because man's will is not free; they had to move in this direction for satisfaction, and only when these principles are thoroughly understood by all mankind will this great transition come about. Now, let me get back to our school children."

"Just one second. Now I can understand why a driving school will not graduate a student. He will go as long as he thinks it is necessary, but the decision as to when he is ready to leave and tackle the real thing is his and his alone to make."

"You do understand. The same thing applies when it is time to leave school. As our children become teenagers, they will want to prepare themselves for earning a living and for marriage. They will be shown everything that is known on how to arouse and satisfy sexual passion, without shame or modesty, and the parents will never have anything to fear. They will look over the many ways of earning a living and will select the one for which they seem to have a propensity. However, since they will be constantly testing themselves to see if they are qualifying, and if they are not, they may decide to change their course, which is their own business. Because the earth is not unlimited in regard to space, food, and other necessities in relation to the total population that steadily increases... "

"And if you do what you say you're going to do, put an end to all war, crime, etc., the earth would soon be entirely too crowded."

"There will exist in the International Bureau of Welfare a group of scientists from each nation who, like parents guiding their children without blame, will recommend what is required to sustain and improve the world's standard of living (such as how many offspring should a couple aim for), but since there will be no criticism should this not be heeded, everyone will desire to abide by these recommendations for fear they might be responsible for hurting those whom they know must excuse what cannot be justified."

"But this will come in conflict with certain religions that teach otherwise."

"So does teaching that man's will is not free. But religion gets completely displaced only because God has no further need for its services. Of what value is having an organization that asks mankind to have faith in God, to have faith that one day he will reveal himself to be a reality, when he does this by delivering us from all evil?"

"There is a great humor to all this."

"No question about it."

"But there is one thing that puzzles me about school. If a boy leaves before he has selected some kind of trade or profession to study for, because he finds it too difficult and ends up taking a job as a laborer, are you going to tell me that his job is just as important as that of a brain surgeon? Is it possible to show him the same amount of respect, and wouldn't people in general consider him uneducated in comparison?"

"I will show you that he will not be respected less, or the brain surgeon more; that his job will not be considered less important; and that he will be judged just as educated as anybody else."

"I don't believe it is possible to do this... No, I don't want to bet, just show me."

"Take a look at the pictures of these two girls and tell me which one you consider more beautiful?"

"You told me, and I understood that words like beautiful are going to become obsolete, so I can't tell you which is more beautiful, but I can tell you which one appeals to me more. Are you trying to tell me that the word education will become obsolete for the same reason?"

"That's exactly right."

"But there is quite a difference. A person cannot help being born with the features she has, but education can be acquired."

"Did you understand when I explained how the brain projects words as slides onto a screen of differences?"

"I understood perfectly."

"Well then, you would know that for any word to be symbolic of something real, we must be able to see the reality through the symbol. We see cat, mouse, rat, dog, tree, apple, orange, sun, moon, book, male, female, etc., all through the symbols, but can you see a beautiful girl or an educated one through word symbols?"

"I don't know about you, but Elizabeth Taylor looks beautiful to me."

"Suppose someone else says she is not beautiful to him? Judges at a beauty contest don't all agree, and in some parts of the world low hanging breasts, a huge rear end, and big fat thighs are considered the ideal. Now, if I draw a picture of a dog and put the word dog right next to it, no one will say the symbol is inaccurate because it is not, but try to do the same thing with the words 'education' and 'beautiful.' These are projected upon this screen of differences, and then when you see these differences with your eyes, it appears that they exist as part of the external world because they are circumscribed with the word."

"I told you I understand all that."

"However... be patient, these words also project a value as existing externally, as if the world is divided up into stratified layers of importance, but value is a relation between you and something else. You may like one girl better than another, but this is your preference. However, when you say she is beautiful or educated, then you are saying she contains a value that other girls do not have, and you have placed them in a definite position of inferiority. Because of the belief that this external value called education is a part of the real world, you will hear one boy say, 'I am more educated than both of you because I finished college.' The doctors of philosophy, and those with additional titles, say, 'We are more educated than all of you put together.' And finally Will Durant, resenting Spencer's conception of education 'as the adjustment of the individual to his environment,' which he considered a 'dead, mechanical definition that resulted in the conquest of our schools by mechanical and theoretical science, to the comparative exclusion of such 'useless' subjects as literature, history, philosophy and art,' and not wishing to put himself on the same level as those professors who had not expanded their horizon to the extent that he and Edward Gibbon had done, defined education to include him and exclude most of them, for he wrote: 'Education does not mean that we have become certified experts in business, or mining, or botany, or journalism, or epistemology; it means that through the absorption of the moral, intellectual and esthetic inheritances of our race we have come to understand and control ourselves as well as the external world; that we have chosen the best as our associates both in spirit and in the flesh; that we have learned to add courtesy to culture, wisdom to knowledge, and forgiveness to understanding. When will our colleges produce such men?' You see, as far as he is concerned, college does not produce an educated man, and that is why he was disliked by a great many professors."

"I don't think he would like you either if you told him he was not an educated man, nor would Elizabeth Taylor like to be told she is not a beautiful woman."

"But there is a big difference. I am not taking anything away from them because nobody will be considered beautiful or educated. Just because one person decides to read a lot of books, while someone else does not, is no reason to say the former has greater value. In reality, Spencer's conception was accurate because he was not creating any greater value for what each person preferred to do over another. It was each individual's adjustment to his environment. Therefore, what is the need to have a word that applies to everybody, regardless of what they choose to do with their time? If one man prefers to read 100 books and another 20 books and a third none at all, the only thing we can say without placing anyone in a position of inferiority, which is a hurt, is that some people like to read and study more than others. Durant, extending the definition to include other differences, writes: 'It should develop every creative power in him, and open his mind to all the enjoyable and instructive aspects of the world. A man who is heavy with millions, but to whom Beethoven or Corot or Hardy, or the glow of the autumn woods in the setting sun, is only sound and color signifying nothing, is merely the raw material of a man.'"

"Something struck me that I think is very funny. If people are denied the satisfaction of trying to put down others by asking questions the answers of which are already known to them, a great many subjects will not be studied because these are imposed by the school only; the student is compelled to choose between A and B when he prefers neither. In other words, if someone memorized an entire encyclopedia, the only way he could use this knowledge is if some person asked him questions, which wouldn't be likely when a library is available along with teachers who are paid to answer questions (and I just remembered, he wouldn't be asked as this would be a form of advance blame just as long as the answer could be gotten without disturbing him, as I could have done regarding my question about the time). This means that only the subjects necessary to earn a living, or those books and other things that give pleasure in themselves, will be pursued."

"Very good. What you have just said is this: How is it humanly possible for any person to desire spending years lifting heavy weights for the purpose of developing huge muscles so he can show off his physique when he knows that he will be shipwrecked on an island where nobody will ever see him?"

"But some people read heavy books not to acquire information but to develop a huge vocabulary which is used in daily conversation and to express themselves better."

"This is their business, as is anything they choose to do. Remember, nobody will ever tell them what to do. But let me show you something very humorous when Durant's definition of an educated man is paraphrased by comparison.

In the new world, we are able to control and understand ourselves as well as the external world, not because we have absorbed the 'moral, intellectual and esthetic inheritances of our race,' but only because we know at last what it means that man's will is not free. 'We have chosen the best as our associates both in spirit and in the flesh,' only because the knowledge that we will never be criticized, ridiculed, blamed or punished, allows us, for the very first time, to select what is truly best for ourselves even though we may prefer rock and roll to Beethoven, Zane Grey to Shakespeare, Elvis Presley to Caruso, the atmosphere of a poolroom to the 'glow of the autumn woods in the setting sun,' or a laborer as a friend to an author, philosopher, historian or piano virtuoso. 'We have learned to add courtesy to culture, and wisdom to knowledge' only because we have finally learned what wisdom really is, which makes it impossible to be discourteous. And we have added 'forgiveness to understanding' only because we know that man is truly not to blame, which gives us the understanding to know how to prevent from coming back into existence that for which forgiveness was previously necessary. 'When will our' present environment 'produce such men?'"

"I really liked that, Larry! But I believe we will have to wait until the new world before such people can be produced. I still can't see, though, why a person earning more money and working at a job that requires much more development of his mind, would not get greater respect than, let us say, a laborer, even if the word education is done away with."

"You are confusing preference with respect. You are saying that if someone discovers he is incapable of earning the kind of money that would set himself apart from others, you can't respect him as much, but all you are actually saying is that if you had a choice, you would prefer associating with one type of individual rather than with another, and there is nothing wrong with that because nobody is getting hurt. But when you consider one person more important not because of his value to you, but only because you have judged the world in stratified layers of importance, then when an individual climbs to the top, he is the most important person alive. If it were you who had climbed to the very top and were now judged the Champion of Importance, would it be possible for you to say, of another, that he is as important as you? If you are the champion pool player, is it possible to point to another and say he is the champion?"

"I agree that this couldn't be done."

"When you use words that give to someone greater importance than another, you automatically place yourself in a relation of lesser importance, lesser respect. Consequently, by raising others you lower yourself; by lowering others you raise yourself. Since it is impossible to desire lowering others when you know this will be a concrete hurt for which there would be no blame, and since it is impossible to desire raising others when you know this is a hurt to yourself, you are given no choice but to remove all words that do this very thing, giving to all mankind a perfectly balanced equation of mutual respect."

"But something still doesn't seem just right. Do you think a person would study for years and years if it were not for the distinguishing titles bestowed upon him... Sir... Doctor... Professor... etc.? He likes this respect, and he worked hard to get it."

"He will study whatever he desires for the purpose of earning a living and anything else he might have in mind, but not to make himself more important and deserving of greater respect. Gibbon became famous for The Decline and Fall of the Roman Empire, as did Durant for The Story of Civilization, but this doesn't entitle them to greater respect."

"But there is certainly a big difference between these men and those who should never learn to read or write."

"That's true, there is a difference, and that difference is that the two of them preferred reading a lot of books and studying so that one day they might write something and become famous, while the others preferred not going to school at all. It is true that they recognized certain talents and developed these, while the others, not having these, were not motivated in that direction, but it was only because certain words came into existence..."

"Out of necessity, right?"

"Right... that they were made to feel inferior. It was this projection of value onto a screen of differences that created a feeling of importance and of deserving greater respect."

"But these differences also separated those who did not want to be friendly from those who did. A doctor doesn't want just anybody calling him by his first name, nor does a professor. You've heard the expression 'Familiarity breeds contempt.' Suppose a student addressed his professor, 'Hi, Harry!' or a child his father, 'Hi Oscar!'"

"You must remember that these things are a sign of disrespect and unwanted familiarity in our present world. If you do not like the name given to you upon your birth, and wish to be called by another, this is your business. However, you cannot demand its use because this is a judgment of what is right for someone else. But if the name does not create an atmosphere of disrespect, there is no reason the name you pick for yourself should not be used by others. If, for example, you prefer to teach your child to call you Dad instead of Harry, there is nothing wrong with that, just as long as you don't deny your son the right to call you Harry because you feel it is a sign of disrespect. In our present world, this would definitely be considered a sign, but in the new world it would not, and because it would not, a boy might prefer calling his male parent Dad because Dad prefers it."

"I think I understand now. If a man desires his students to call him teacher, professor, Harry, Smith, or what have you, there is no reason for them to object unless he is trying to exact more respect than he is prepared to give. In other words, if he said to his students, 'I expect everyone to address me as Sir,' but denied the young males in his class the same privilege when he addressed them, then an unbalanced equation of respect is created. This brings to mind how I changed from calling my uncle, Uncle Monroe, to just Monroe when I got much older and felt this inequality."

"However, the reason these distinguishing names of respect came into existence was only because there was so much disrespect unconsciously imposed by words. Away from home, parents, uncles and aunts were abused, ridiculed, criticized, and blamed for so many things that it was a source of satisfaction to be called Dad, Mom, Uncle, and Aunt, for this meant that the children were looking up to them with at least this amount of respect. But when Dad returns from work in the new world, and his son says, 'Hi Larry!' or 'Hi Dad!', there will be no disrespect whatsoever."

"But what about the various menial services like a maid, butler, street cleaner, garbage collector, etc.?"

"Again, you can see the disrespect in the word menial, but the same principle applies regardless. However, many services will come to an end, street cleaning for one. How is it possible for you to throw trash in the street, which then makes it necessary to employ street cleaners, when you know this will be a hurt to the taxpayers who will never blame you for doing what you know they must excuse, and you cannot justify? And when parents and children make their own beds, wash their own dishes, throw out their own trash, etc., there will never be any reason for them not to honor and respect each other. Finally, children will go to school not to acquire an education, not to become learned, cultured, mature, refined (these are all words that judge others as less important and therefore deserving of less respect), but only to learn what they want to, not what others think they should."

Chapter 6
THE DISPLACED

"I take for granted you are finished discussing the new school system and are now ready to demonstrate how to do what seems virtually impossible, even though I understand all that you have shown me so far and agree with the relations."

"With our basic principle to guide us, together with advance blame, it is really not such a big thing to put a permanent end to war, crime, inflation, and all the other evils of our economic world. Therefore, assuming that you fully understand what it means that man's will is not free, the next step is to remove from around the entire earth, regardless of who gets displaced, all those people who are in any way associated with blame. Consequently, since all armed forces of defense blame in advance the possibility of being attacked, they must be displaced. And since it is mathematically impossible for armies of offense to desire to drop bombs on those who refuse to retaliate under the new conditions, they too have no reason to remain in existence."

"Does this also apply within a nation?"

"Absolutely. When all the police forces are removed, assuring every potential thief that no one henceforth will ever stand in their way of taking whatever they want (if they will want to when I am through with them), then there is absolutely no need whatever for armed weapons?"

"There is no need, I agree, for a potential criminal to use a gun if he knows with certainty that no one will stand in his way."

"This displaces all judges, private eyes, floor walkers, armored trucks, vaults, burglar alarms; all things that are locked will be unlocked, and all things used to check on a person's honesty, such as a cash register to check the cashier, as well as the latter, will also be displaced. Lawyers, politicians, governors, mayors, the President and Vice President, ambassadors, diplomats, everybody notwithstanding, get displaced if their manner of earning a living is the least bit redolent of blame. This also includes direct salespeople who knock on doors and telephone solicitors, as well as those who approach the buyer. The relation between a seller and buyer is the same as between a husband and wife. If someone is interested in buying something, he will extend an invitation, and then only will he be talked to. Also displaced are all collection and credit investigating agencies and all employment agencies because the first blames someone for not paying his bills, the second checks him in advance to see if he will, and the third tries to screen applicants, which blames them for being dishonest about their qualifications."

"A great many employers are not looking for Jews, Blacks, etc., and the agency screens this aspect also."

"Whatever the reason, since blame is present in some form, these agencies get displaced. All beauty contests come to an end; all those who make their living by asking for donations also get displaced because they are asking for a favor, and all critics — those who tell the world their opinion of a picture or play, as well as censors, another form of critic — get displaced. Everything the government manufactures for the purpose of granting someone a license to do something, and all personnel engaged in this aspect, are displaced. If someone wishes to identify their car so it does not get confused with others like it, they will put their nameplate on it. Even the collection of taxes, as it now exists, comes to an end because this blames people for not paying."

"Are you telling me that a person will pay what he wants to pay?"

"Not exactly, but if someone doesn't want to pay, there will be no one forcing him. However, the new tax system will be explained shortly."

"I still don't quite understand about salespeople."

"If A, the salesperson, approaches B, he is expressing his desire to sell something without considering the possibility that B does not want to be annoyed. When he realizes that this is an annoyance for which he will never be criticized, he will lose his desire and will approach B only when invited to do so. Even in a department store, when a salesperson approaches a potential buyer, the same thing occurs, but in the new world, only the buyers will make the first move."

"Suppose the buyer, after making this first contact and trying on a dress, says to the salesgirl, 'How does it look on me?'"

"She will never ask. This was already explained, remember? The department stores will only need fitters where certain clothes are concerned."

"Between those you are displacing in the government and in private industry, there are not too many left."

"I'm not finished yet. The biggest item to be displaced, and one that will come as a complete surprise, is the material aspect of money itself, not its purchasing power, for this demonstrates an obvious distrust of people's honesty by denying them an opportunity to spend more than they can show cash or credit for. But let me show in greater detail why this material aspect must come to an end."

"Are you sure you're not kidding me? Do you mean that the green stuff we passed to each other so many times across a pool table is definitely coming to an end? I can just see some pool hustlers I know turning it in — for what? And I would like to see Charlie's expression... Gee! I forgot to pick him up when I came over."

"Don't worry about it. I'll give him a copy of the book when it is published so he can study everything."

"I sure would like to see the expression on his face when he hears that money, as a medium of exchange, is coming to an end. Well, continue."

"Anyway, when no one will ever blame what you do, permitting you to steal all you want — if you want to; when no one will ever check on your honesty in any way, the present manner of paying for things becomes obsolete. Instead of having a cashier check your purchases, receive your money, and give you change, you could do this yourself. Certainly, you can put a one-dollar bill in a drawer and take a twenty out, but if it is food you want, why even bother with the cash when you could clean out the store — if you want to. Nobody is going to stop you, check to see if you paid for this merchandise, or question your honesty in any way. Consequently, what difference does it make whether you use this material aspect of money or slips of paper on which you record the amount you are spending? What difference does it make whether you receive cash, a check, or a slip of paper on payday representing the purchasing power for your labor? What difference does it make to a businessman whether he deposits $2000 cash and checks in the bank or records the total receipts in a book, throwing away the slips of paper? He is interested, like the rest of us, in what this money represents, its purchasing power. Therefore, when the slips of paper are thrown away, it makes no difference to him, just so long as his purchasing power is not impaired. What difference would it make to you, Jim, whether you go up to a cash drawer and pay for the little things you buy with a $20 bill, taking your own change, or whether you write $18.50 on a slip of paper, put this in the drawer and deduct the amount from your total cash reserve, just as you do with a checking account? What difference would it make whether you mail a check to pay a bill or a slip of paper, just so your creditor acknowledges receipt of this, so you can deduct while he adds? What difference would it make whether you put a 25-cent postage stamp on an envelope and then deduct while the Post Office adds?"

"It would make a helluva difference if the people would desire to take advantage of this opportunity to steal. But isn't this somewhat like the honor system used in certain universities?"

"Of course not, because if a student does not live up to the established code of ethics, he is severely censured, in many cases expelled, whereas here we know that man is not to blame for hurting others because his will is not free — we are back to the basic principle which I take for granted you understand. As for the desire to take advantage of this opportunity to steal, you must constantly bear in mind that in order to prevent this desire from ever arising, it is first absolutely necessary to remove all the forces that try in some way, through threats of punishment and retaliation, to prevent us from being hurt by others."

"But this would give our counterfeiters, thieves, and bank robbers a ball."

"If they will desire to steal when I am through with them... and I'm far from through.

"Now, another change that will lay off millions more people is the result of competition between nations, and within those countries that are capitalistic. Let me show you what I mean.

At the present time, the United States is in desperate need of foreign markets, as is Russia, but to a lesser degree. The latter seeks to exchange its surpluses for the purpose of maintaining and improving its standard of living; for the former, if its products are not sold, it is faced with laying off millions of workers until a chain reaction depression could cripple the economy of the nation. Consequently, the government must do everything humanly possible to keep these ports open, and when communism threatens to close them sooner or later, war is inevitable as the lesser of two evils. Furthermore, various things cause prices to rise, which occasions the unions (they also get displaced) to force wage increases to satisfy the difference, but when the stockholders see a decrease in their dividends, they raise prices to adjust this difference. It's a vicious cycle. Anyway, when these ports are thrown open, competition between all the countries will become extremely keen, and millions more will be laid off when the various manufacturers find their products are not moving."

"Stop already, Larry! You have half the population of the world unemployed. The question is, what are you going to do about it?"

"The answer is very simple. When the transition takes place, each working individual will have attained a standard of living that can be measured in dollars and cents. For example, if a person brings home after taxes, $150 a week, but only uses $125 because the rest he saves, then his standard of living would be the latter figure. Consequently, if he had as little as one penny in purchasing power taken away from him by the economy, he would be blamed for having too much money, and since he would never blame this hurt because he knows it cannot be helped, when I know it can be without hurting anyone, that is, without taking one penny away from anybody's standard of living in the entire world, I am going to prevent what can no longer be justified."

"If you can do that, then I'll know you were sent here from another planet."

"If you understand the basic principle and how it is extended, you should be able to do this yourself."

"Never mind; you show me."

"To understand how, it is important to know that when a person loses his job involuntarily for one reason or another, he is not considered displaced until he has used up all his reserve cash, but when he is at this point and still cannot find a job, he will draw the amount of money required to sustain his standard of living from the Bureau of Internal Revenue by entering this $125, as an example, in his cash reserve record book, and then send a notice of this transaction so it can be deducted."

"But what's stopping him from taking more than this amount?"

"The realization that, should he take more, he would be hurting the very people who now are not hurting him in any way and who would never blame him, no matter how much he took, because he knows they must excuse everything he does. Consequently, he is compelled to prefer being absolutely honest with himself and others, for this is the only avenue open for needed satisfaction. This same principle compels him to look for a job immediately, unless he still has money of his own, but no one will tell him where or when to work, in any country, because there is no need to under the changed conditions."

"But suppose he can't find a job paying the amount necessary to meet his standard of living?"

"He will simply draw the difference from the Bureau."

"But suppose an employer, knowing this, deliberately pays his new employees less?"

"How is it possible for him to do this when he knows he would never be blamed for stealing this money from the taxpayers? It's the same principle again and again."

"But suppose the person displaced was a hired killer whose standard of living was $100,000 a year?"

"It would make no difference because we are all God's children, and the same principle would apply."

"Are you trying to tell me that nobody in the world who understands what it means that man's will is not free would be able to cheat under those conditions?"

"Could you?"

"No, I couldn't."

"Well, stop worrying about the others. You only have to use your personal experience as a guinea pig test and know that their nature is no different than yours. Once the transition gets under way you will have only your own business to concern yourself with."

"But wouldn't this cause a tremendous increase in taxation? And how does the guarantee affect an entire nation that might fall short in the actual products to sustain this standard of living?"

"If Russia, for example, needed to exchange certain surplus products in order to maintain her own standard of living but was unable because some other country beat her out in the competition, all she would have to do..."

(Or any country — no partiality)

"...is draw the amount of money required to sustain her own standard of living from the International Bureau of Internal Revenue by entering this amount in her record book, ordering and paying for in cash what is needed from any seller of her choice, and then sending a record of this amount to the Bureau so it can be deducted."

"This is all very well, but what about taxation?"

"Every week, the Bureau in each country will issue a statement as to what percent of a person's income is required to meet the bill, and if it happens to be 5%, and your income is $200, you would remit a slip of paper for $10 and deduct this from your cash reserve. But if the tax makes you go below your standard, you would only send in the amount that does not go below. However, if a country cannot back up a standard of living because the products necessary are not available in sufficient quantity — and no matter what is done within the country, these cannot be gotten in sufficient quantity — then and then only would a nation draw the necessary funds from the International Bureau, as described. And each and every week, this Bureau would also make an announcement to all the countries that a certain percentage of a person's income would be required to meet the bill, and no one would object because no one is getting hurt by going below their accustomed standard. Furthermore, any seller who would increase prices and any employee who would force a wage increase would be stealing from the taxpayers because many people would have to draw an additional amount in order to meet their standard of living as a consequence of these increases. Since it cannot satisfy a person to steal when he knows he will not be blamed in any way, and when he also knows that no one is now hurting him, all prices are prevented from being raised, which breaks the vicious cycle and puts a permanent end to inflation."

"But if an employee cannot increase his salary..."

"I said he cannot force an increase. The boss might wish to give him a raise or a bonus. But regardless of this, a change will take place as a consequence that will make everybody much happier and wealthier. Remember, when millions upon millions of people lose their accustomed manner of earning a living, there will be more labor available than can be readily imagined. Since everybody will desire to spend as never before because of the guarantee, this will result in a tremendous boon that will not only employ just about all the unemployed, reducing the need for unemployment compensation (taxes), but will give the investors, the builders, the brains, the greatest opportunity imaginable. What is of greatest importance is the fact that since prices cannot be raised and competition will exist greater than ever before, they can only go in one direction — down. And what is of still greater significance is this: In due time, more and more people will get laid off because less and less need to buy what they already have. There is a limit to the number of material things a person can own. And when this time comes, they will have no need for this money. In other words, if you spend your money, others will receive it in the form of income. If you have nothing on which to spend and nothing in which to invest, they will receive it in the form of taxes. What you do with it is your business, and have I given you a choice?"

"This whole thing is absolutely fantastic, Larry; it really is! Under these conditions, the only difference between a communist and a capitalist country is that the latter has a lot of corporations while the former has only one. But the amazing thing is that when workers get laid off in either country, what they do is exactly the same, that is, look for something else to do without anybody dictating; and if they are unable to find work because there isn't any, they would simply take a vacation until called back by drawing the money to sustain their standard of living... from the Bureau, as you explained. But how does this new way of life affect insurance companies, advertising, gambling, selling dope, the lending of money, etc.? And what about all the deals that are made under contract?"

"There will be no more contracts drawn up where people are bound by a legal entity, but there will be written or oral contracts to clarify the responsibilities of the parties involved in a particular deal. For the very first time, businesspeople will refrain from trying to put something over on the buyer. Consequently, complete honesty will be the policy. Advertising companies will be absolutely certain that what they say on the air, in the newspapers, magazines, etc., is the truth and nothing but the truth. If something is definitely the cause of cancer, then let it be known, but if it is not, if it is just an association, then the Cancer Society had better do more research before an announcement is made."

"Insurance premiums and interest rates will come down to such a degree because of the guarantee that everybody will be able to afford both, and the applicants will never be questioned as to their ability to pay. As for the selling of dope and gambling, the latter is a legitimate business because nobody makes an individual gamble unless he wants to. However, when a person knows that, should he lose beyond what he can afford, this would be a hurt to his family, who would never blame him for this, he is prevented from going over his limit. As for the sale of anything that could be harmful, the most the seller can do is make this known; the rest is up to the buyer. If a yogi decides to sit on a flagpole and falls off, breaking his skull, the most we can do is bury him."

"I'm sure glad you called the bet off. This entire blueprint you have drawn up is absolutely infallible, and its fulfillment must come into existence sooner or later because it is the direction mankind is compelled to travel for needed satisfaction when it is finally known what it means that man's will is not free."

"Very well said, Jim. This is nothing but God's will."

"Why do you constantly refer to God when I know you are not a religious person?"

"Mathematical proof that he is a reality has just been demonstrated. This new world is coming into existence not because of my will, not because I made a discovery (sooner or later it had to be discovered by someone because the knowledge of what it means that man's will is not free is a definite part of the real world), but only because we have no choice. Do you really think the solar system came into existence by accident? Do you think it was an accident that the sun is just the proper distance from the earth, so we don't roast or freeze, or an accident that the earth revolves just at the proper speed to fulfill many exacting functions? Do you think it was an accident that our brains and bodies developed just that way? Do you think it was an accident that I made my discovery when I did? You should hear how I made it; you wouldn't believe what I had to go through."

"Can you tell me about it?"

"Some other time. To show you how fantastic is the infinite wisdom that directs every aspect of this universe, which includes the solar and mankind systems through invariable laws that we are at last getting to understand, just follow this: Here is versatile man: writer, composer, artist, inventor, scientist, philosopher, theologian, architect, builder, mathematician, chess player, murderer, prostitute, thief, etc., whose will is absolutely and positively not free despite all the learned opinions to the contrary, yet compelled by his very nature to believe that it is since it was impossible not to blame and punish the terrible evils that came into existence out of necessity, and then permitted, after reaching a sufficient degree of development, to perceive the necessary relations as to why will is not free and what this means for the entire world, which perception was utterly impossible without the development, and absolutely necessary for the inception of our Golden Age. Where in all history have you ever heard anything more incredible?"

"Nowhere, I'm sure. To think, mankind has been growing and developing just like a child from infancy. There is no way a baby can go from birth to old age without passing through the necessary steps, and from what I have just learned, there is no way man could have reached this turning point in his life without also going through the necessary steps. But what surprises me no end is that I have never detected a note of pride in your voice, not the least bit, and here you made one of the most fantastic discoveries."

"How is it possible for me to be proud when I know for a certainty that my will is not free. I didn't ask to be born, and I was compelled to move in a particular direction for needed satisfaction. The only difference between us is that I am me, and you are you."

"My only complaint is that I might not be living when this new world becomes a reality, and it really isn't fair when you think of how many billions of people suffered and died to help develop it for others to enjoy."

"I told you I have quite a surprise in store. Just be patient."

Chapter 7
IMMORTALITY

"So now, you are going to put the icing on the cake, is that right?"

"I suppose you could call it that."

"And if my memory hasn't failed me, you are going to reveal something about death in a mathematical manner that is supposed to make me very happy, correct?"

"That is correct."

"This will have nothing to do with a spiritual world of souls?"

"Right."

"And I take for granted you will not be able to use the basic principle here, true?"

"Although it has been an infallible guide and miraculous catalyst through the labyrinths of human relations, it cannot assist me here; but it did not help other scientists discover atomic energy, nor was it used to reveal itself. However, that of which it is composed, this perception of undeniable relations that escapes the average eye, will take us by the hand and demonstrate, in a manner no one will be able to deny, that there is absolutely nothing to fear in death not only because it is impossible for us to regret it, but primarily because (now don't jump to any conclusions when you hear what I'm about to say) — we will be born again and again and again."

"No wonder you checked me."

"But this does not mean what you might think it means, because the life you live and are conscious of right now has no relation whatsoever to you and your consciousness in another life."

"This is confusing. I'm conscious now, and I know nothing of a consciousness in another life."

"I realize that, but to help me explain it, I shall begin by asking you a very important question. Doesn't it seem rather strange to you that of all the millions of years the earth has been in existence, you, of all people, should be born at this time to see the wonders of the world and the inception of the Golden Age? Why weren't you born back in the time of Socrates, or why shouldn't you be born later on after the transition has been officially launched?"

"I was born now simply because my father met my mother, fell in love, and got married. They gave birth to four children, and I am the third of the four."

"This is all very true, but it doesn't reveal a deeper truth. Does matter itself reveal atomic energy? Do the individual planets, moon, and sun reveal the solar system, unless you look into this deeply? Do individual people reveal the mankind system? Does all of it together reveal the reality of God unless certain mathematical relations are perceived?

Certainly, your mother and father got married and had four children, but this tells us nothing about the laws that are necessary to understand in order to know why there is nothing to fear in death. At one time, we were afraid of thunder and lightning, thinking it was the wrath of God, but now we don't fear the thunder and try to protect ourselves as best we can against the lightning. Until man discovered the cause of an eclipse, he was afraid that something terrible was going to happen. This became an ominous sign that was blamed for whatever evil followed."

"I agree that my answer was rather superficial, and I also agree that it does seem rather strange that I was born now with all these millions of years the earth has been in existence. But strange as it seems, it really means nothing to me and doesn't stop me from having a horrible fear of death."

"Now the actual reason it is not strange that you are conscious now (I shall prove this, remember), is simply because you, no one else (that is, not you as you now are, but you as someone else), will always be conscious as long as mankind exists."

"And you are going to prove this in a mathematical, undeniable manner! You can't be serious!"

"Would you like to bet that $50,000 again?"

"What's the use of betting; you won't take it if you win. But I still think it's impossible... with reservations, that is, after your blueprint performance. Well, show me; seeing is believing."

"The first step is to establish certain undeniable facts. So tell me, is there such a thing as the past? Does this word symbolize something that is a part of the real world?"

"Of course. Yesterday was Thursday, and there isn't any person alive who will disagree."

"I, too, will agree with that, but this does not prove whether the word 'past' is an accurate symbol. Can you take it, like you can the words apple and pear, and hang it up on something so I can look through it at the real McCoy?"

"You know that's impossible to do, so why do you ask?"

"In order for me to prove what seems impossible, it is absolutely necessary that I deconfuse your mind so we can communicate with each other. Now, the reason man cannot do what I asked is because there is no such thing as the past. All we have, in reality, is the present. Our brain is divided into compartments, and in the memory section are innumerable word slides on which our experiences are recorded. A second ago, yesterday, last week, last month, two years ago, two thousand years ago, are slides in our brain projector through which we see how many times, or what portion of one time, the earth revolves on its axis, but if we were not able to remember (store away these slides), the word 'past' would never have come into existence because we are born, grow old, and die... all in the present. Everything that you can possibly do, from the time you get up to the time you go to bed, and even your sleep, is done in the present, as is the shining of the sun. Are we in agreement?"

"I understand what you mean, and I cannot disagree; so continue."

"The next fact to be established, and the most important, is to realize that it is mathematically impossible to see this world through any consciousness but your own. It is your eyes through which your brain looks out, not those of someone else. This is why you are conscious right at this moment, and why you will be conscious a hundred and a million years from now."

"When you say I will be conscious many years from now in the future, you certainly don't mean this particular body, right?"

"Correct."

"And when you say I can't see this world through any consciousness but my own, others are conscious too, correct? And what if I was knocked unconscious?"

"It is true that others are conscious while you are, but you observe this through your consciousness. As for being knocked unconscious, you would then be only sleeping, not dead, and we are dealing with death, not sleep."

"In that case, I understand, and again I must agree."

"Now, let us imagine that your mother and father, Adam and Eve, gave birth to ten children. You, me, Mary, Harry, Charlie, Inez, Sue..."

"Is that the boy named Sue?"

"Don't be funny; one boy named Sue is enough. Anyway, Linda, Janis, Madeline. Through the course of nature, these children, not knowing anything about incest, got married. Mary with Harry, me and Madeline, you with Inez, Charlie with Janis . . ."

"But that only leaves Sue and Linda."

"Then Sue must be the boy named Sue. Through the course of time, these ten gave birth to 40 more children, and those 40 gave birth to another 150 until the earth's total population was all of two hundred two. However, Adam, by now, is a very old man and about to die, but just before passing away, he says to me, 'Larry, isn't it strange that with all the years the earth has been in existence, I am conscious right now of this world? I am conscious of you, my wife, your brothers and sisters, and all the rest in our family. When the last baby was born on my 100th birthday, I said to myself, 'Wouldn't it be wonderful if that were me, starting life all over again so that I could enjoy the sun, the stars, and all the other things for another 100 years? But I know it couldn't be me because this is me, talking to you, and number 202 is a tiny infant, while I am worn out with age. It would be wonderful, though, if people didn't have to die, not that I really mind because I've long since forgotten what it's like to make love; but if I could be born again with a completely new body it would be heaven on earth; and maybe in my new life there would be something made to cover my feet so they don't get all cut up from walking on small pieces of broken stone.'"

"I have great news, Adam, because your wish is about to come true, but it is important to understand that just as long as you are living, any person born cannot possibly be you. However, when you die, this you, this bubble of consciousness, is gone, which makes it impossible for a newborn child to have any relation to you but only to those still living, who refer to this baby as him or her when they have something to say. Now answer me very carefully; if you admit (remember, Adam, we agreed on certain facts) it is mathematically impossible to see this universe through any consciousness but your own, then when you die and are no longer here to see this world, who will possess this next bubble of consciousness?"

"If it is a boy, he will possess it. If a girl, she will."

"But how is it possible for you to say this when you are no longer here to say it, for this expression must pass through your consciousness, and you know it is not your consciousness because you have just died; so whose consciousness are we talking about?"

"I've seen a lot of babies born (it's true I haven't seen anyone die yet), but I can't imagine how a child born after my death could be me."

"If it is mathematically impossible for you to say 'his or her consciousness' regarding this infant that was conceived after your death and who was just delivered, because this must have reference to your consciousness, and your consciousness isn't here since you just died; and since the other 201 people in your family have their own consciousness; and since it is mathematically impossible for you to see this universe through any consciousness but your own (this was already established as an undeniable fact), then this new child must contain your consciousness, the consciousness of number 202."

"Larry, you actually did it! You're a hundred percent right! This is the most wonderful news! But if I tried to explain this to someone else, Charlie, for example, he just might not understand. Isn't there a way to clarify it?"

"Suppose we let A represent all the sperm, and B all the ova pertaining to mankind, while the combination of one with the other will be designated C, which is you, your potential consciousness of existence. Let us further suppose that A joins up with B, and during their uterine journey, you, C, end up as a miscarriage, which means that you just died. Consequently, you are not conscious of your existence because your body was never born to give you this, and therefore, the relation expressed in these words, 'he died, she died, or it died,' would have no meaning where you are concerned because you just died, and your existence is absolutely necessary for the relation.

Now, this potential mother and father still want their first baby; they want you, which word symbolizes human living substance, so they try again, but this time you are born, only one month later, you die of a heart attack after taking a good look at your father. But still persistent, and having a lot of fun, this boy and girl, who want you very much, try again with viable success; but 18 years later, you end up in a hospital where you die. Much older now, but still capable of propagating, mom and dad are not satisfied to lose you, so they try once more to bring you into existence. Now, in actual reality, though hereditary differences exist between the three C's, the word you is a designation only for the viable substance that comes into the world and is identified with a name to establish these differences, which mom and dad grow to love. But what is the difference between the potential 'you' who died during the uterine journey, the 'you' who died one month after birth, or the 'you' who died 18 years later? Because you are conscious of your existence and individuality during those years in the present, write a book, build a home, make a lot of friends who cry when you die, doesn't take away from the fact that you are a combination of A and B, which continues in existence even while you are alive and regardless of what happens to C. If you had died a hundred thousand times in the uterus of somebody, eventually you, which is a word describing the consciousness of differences about yourself and the fulfillment of your parents' desire to have you, would have been born. Consequently, the consciousness of your individuality, without understanding that you are not only C, which represents the hereditary differences that die, but A and B, which never die because they are carried along from generation to generation and when united develop into any C, makes you perceive an improper relation."

"I don't perceive anything. You are confusing me."

"Simply because the entelechy of A and B develops into the consciousness of C, which permits the recognition of individuality, doesn't negate the substance from which C is derived. Even if all the individual characteristics lie potential in the germplasm, this still has nothing to do with consciousness, which is not an individual characteristic like your face. The word I or you not only reveals this individual difference between yourself and others, but your consciousness of this.

However, now that mom and dad have you, they decide to have another child, and when it is born, it is not you because you already exist. Soon, Mom gives birth to a total of ten. Then, several years later, you got married and gave birth to two children, making a total of 14 in your family. Before long, there were 202 in all. But after reaching a ripe old age of 100 years, you dropped dead from a heart attack, which means that you are no longer here, and that there are only 201 existing in your family. But the children in your family still want you, number 202, so the next child conceived and then born is not two hundred three but you, two hundred two, who will grow, develop, and become conscious of your individuality and existence. However, had you not died, this new child could not possibly be you but him or her in relation to you, although you, 203, will grow, develop, and become conscious of your existence. Remember, the conditions are exactly the same before your birth as after your death. Since you cannot see this world through the consciousness of another, when you die, what consciousness exists belongs to all those living. However, since you are no longer conscious of your existence when dead, and since it is mathematically impossible to see this world through the consciousness of another, only through your own consciousness, and since everybody who is still alive has their own consciousness, it is obvious that the next person conceived and born after your death is not him or her, because this can only be in relation to your consciousness which is not here anymore once you died, but you, not the person who just died, but an individual who grows and develops and becomes conscious of his existence and individuality. Consequently, since there is no such thing as the past, and consciousness can only be your consciousness (never that of another), which can only exist in the present, your consciousness, not your body, will always be here during every moment of time because it is not a personal characteristic like the shape of your nose, but that which applies to the living substance of all mankind."

"The clarification has finally become clear."

"This I or ego that you feel is definitely a reality, for it is you, no one else, that tastes, touches, smells, hears, and sees. But this consciousness is not only an individual thing like the various differences about yourself which we have considered C, but also A and B, the potential consciousness that exists in the germinal substance. Since this substance is that from which your ego, the feel of yourself as an individual, is composed, and since this I or ego is also the conscious expression of this germinal substance, both are one and the same. Consequently, the consciousness of all mankind is the ego, or I, of the total germinal substance which imparts individuality upon the birth of a child, as a tree does to a leaf in the spring of the year. But this all-pervasive consciousness, which exists always in the present (and here's the mathematical solution again), can only be your consciousness because it is mathematically impossible to see this universe through any consciousness but your own. It is this that enables us to say, whether a million years ago or a million years hence, 'Isn't it strange that I was born now to see the wonders of this amazing world?' Consequently, death is a mirage to those who die, and a reality only to the living, and it is our ability to recognize these deeper relations that gives us our knowledge of immortality, our knowledge that we will always be here.

Soon it will dawn on you, as you fully understand these relations, that consciousness is the eternal window of God through which we, all mankind, look out upon this magnificent universe in all its glory and mathematical harmony. It should be further obvious that God can have absolutely no recognition for his existence and achievements unless through the consciousness of man, who is an eternal attribute of God himself. And once it is fully realized that we are the conscious expression of God who exists eternally, simply because there is no such thing as the past or future, only the present, which is eternal, we will become completely conscious of our own eternal life; otherwise, we will be eternal unconsciously.

The perception of these relations makes it obvious that the same general experiences we have gone through of being little boys and girls with a mother and father, growing up, getting married, raising a family in the New World, and remarking about the time way back in the olden days when man used to believe the earth was flat, his will free, and his eyes a sense organ, will continue through eternity because there is no such thing as a beginning and end since time, space, and consciousness are infinite and eternal attributes of the present.

However, when someone dies it is true he is gone and will never return in our lifetime because these relations are also undeniable; but God, through his infinite wisdom, by revealing what it means that man's will is not free, prevents in 90 percent of the cases any premature deaths by eliminating all war, crime, and other forms of hurt that gave rise to a justifiable retaliation, while endowing man with the intelligence to discover the remaining laws that will wipe away the other 10 percent. In our Golden Age, the inception of which will take place very shortly (just as soon as science understands the principles involved) ..."

"That might take 2000 years."

"It might, because this knowledge blinds those who have been looking for a different type of solution, something in accordance with their own opinion. It was the same thing that gave to Mendel posthumous recognition. Anyway, in our Golden Age, the inception of which will take place when all mankind understands the principles involved, we will fall mutually in love, raise a family in complete health, wealth, and security, live to a ripe old age, and die, only to be born for the same happiness again and again and again. Well, you tell me; is God a reality and is he good?"

"This whole thing is so wonderful, Larry, I can't find words to adequately express myself."

"The full realization of what death actually is will destroy the desire to preserve corpses in cemeteries, for this is only a waste of land and the bodies of the deceased. No one will deny that it is sad to lose a loved companion, but satisfaction in

130

preserving this unliving bit of matter can only be gotten when ignorance of the truth engenders the desire."

"All I can do is repeat myself. I can think of no words to adequately express myself. What you have accomplished is absolutely fantastic!"

"In conclusion, Jim, there is something I would like you to always remember. The next time you feel like expressing yourself, whatever you do, don't thank me for pointing the way because my will is not free. Thank God, for it was his wisdom, not mine, that guided us to this Promised Land."

Did you love *View From the Mountaintop: The Vision of Global Harmony*? Then you should read *Inception of the Golden Age: A Scientific Discovery*[1] by Seymour Lessans!

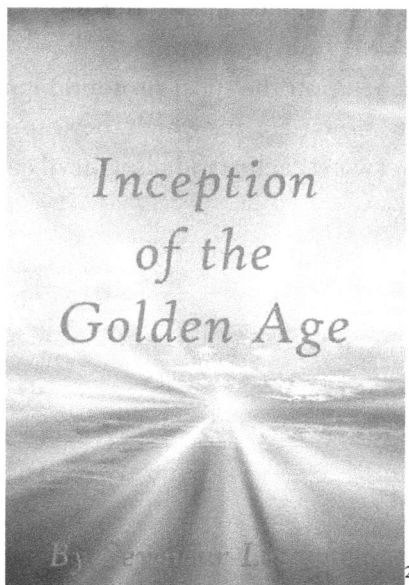

The primary purpose of this book is to reveal a fantastic, scientific discovery about the nature of man whose life, as a direct consequence of this mathematical revelation, will be completely revolutionized in every way for his benefit, bringing about the long awaited Golden Age prophesied in the Bible. However, it is absolutely necessary that you read this book in its entirety, chapter by chapter, in order to understand it, simply because each part is mathematically related to the whole

1. https://books2read.com/u/3Gr0RQ

2. https://books2read.com/u/3Gr0RQ

which presents a solution to every problem of human conduct. Furthermore, so as to preclude your jumping to conclusions, this book has nothing whatever to do with communism, socialism, capitalism, government, religion, philosophy; only with the removal of beliefs among the top echelon of your educated who have been unconsciously passing along from generation to generation the most profound ignorance in the guise of genuine knowledge, for which they cannot be blamed.

Read more at www.declineandfallofallevil.com.

About the Author

Seymour Lessans was born on September 29, 1918 in Newark, New Jersey. He passed away on January 29, 1991. He was the third of four brothers. All through his life he had a tremendous thirst for knowledge, and after many years of extensive reading and careful analysis he made a discovery about the nature of man whose life will be completely revolutionized for his benefit once this discovery is recognized by science. This discovery reveals a natural law which has the power to bring about a new world (the Golden Age of man); a world without war, crime, and all the other evils plaguing mankind.

The rest of his life was devoted to reaching those who could help validate his findings, but he continued to hit stumbling blocks at every turn. His loving wife stood by his side during these difficult years knowing he had a mission to accomplish. Unfortunately, he was unable to bring his discovery to light in his lifetime as he was not a member of a leading university, and held no distinguishing titles. He could not get anyone to listen or to give him the time of day.

His family and all those who knew him will always be inspired by his courage and determination in the midst of incredible odds. His dying words were, "My day will come." He knew he wouldn't be here to see this great change, but he was comforted in the knowledge that no matter how long it took, it would just be a matter of time before this new world becomes a reality. It is with this hope in mind that his life's work (7 books in all from 1961-1988) will be recognized in the 21st century. With everyone's help, it will be possible *in our lifetime* to reach those scientists who can stamp this knowledge with the brevet of truth. This discovery is dedicated to the author, Seymour Lessans, for his incredible contribution to humanity.

Read more at www.declineandfallofallevil.com.